MARKETING WITH WEBINARS

GET NEW CLIENTS IN 1-HOUR PER MONTH

THE EFFICIENT & EFFECTIVE ALTERNATIVE
TO SEMINARS, CONFERENCES & TRADESHOWS

TOM POLAND

Marketing With Webinars

ISBN: 978-0-9775032-6-1

Dedication

To my good friend and constant companion, Red Fox.

Thank you for your wisdom and infallible guidance.

Download the Free Resources Mentioned in This Book

Go to the website below and you'll be able to gain access to a whole vault of valuable resources that I refer to in this book, including:

1. Email samples for inviting prospects to register for a webinar

2. A sample "best practice" webinar registration page

3. A copy of the PowerPoint slides used in a traditional webinar format

4. The exact post-webinar assets I use to double response rates

5. A list of recommended webinar platforms, equipment, and resources

6. A sample marketing calendar

www.MarketingWithWebinars.com

Other helpful links

To interview Tom for your show:
www.InterviewTomPoland.com

To inquire about Tom speaking at your conference email: **support@leadsology.guru**

To check out Tom's main program: **www.iWantSolo.com**

To book a chat with Tom about becoming a client: **www.BookAChatWithTom.com**

Praise For Tom Poland's Marketing Books

TOM POLAND IS ONE OF THE WORLD'S MOST BRILLIANT MARKETERS AND TRAINERS

What a nice treat to see this book! And even better to consume the genius of his system. Tom is very clear and specific in this training. You will understand perfectly what you need to do and not do in order to be successful with your marketing.

I've not found this system anywhere else, in decades of consuming marketing materials.

If you haven't had the success you want in keeping your pipeline full, on a consistent basis, without making yourself crazy... pick this up. It's worth the small investment in yourself and your business.

K.M.
USA

THE NEW WAY TO MARKET

Tom Poland is an absolute genius.

This book thoroughly explains his method. Having read the book and having participated in one of his webinars, I can tell you without question that this is the new way to market.

In particular, it is the new way to market professional services. Tom Poland has gone before and figured out lead generation. I highly recommend his book.

Liam Chrismer
USA

THIS BOOK WILL BE IN DEMAND TOO

A terrific book. With trademark clarity and honesty, Tom Poland shows how to generate a reliable flow of high-quality leads. It's an excellent model and presented with verve and wit.

Richard Koch
Author of *The 80/20 Principle* which sold over one million copies

INGENIOUS

Tom Poland has worked out an innovative and unique process for marketing services, advice, and software as a service.

It is a step-by-step methodology which focuses primarily on one single key marketing tactic which on the surface seems commonplace but which he teaches us to use differently and more effectively.

I spoke to the author on a Zoom call, read his book, and can say with certainty that he is the real deal. The only caveat is that if you don't want to do some of the tasks that are part of his marketing system, then it is probably not for you. Read the book and then you decide. But READ THE BOOK!

Robert W. Bly
New Jersey, USA

PRACTICAL INFORMATION THAT CAN ADD REVENUE FOR YOUR BUSINESS

I a.m. a big fan of Tom Poland. Why? Simply because every time I read one of his books there is at least one idea that increases my revenue. This book continues this great tradition. I strongly urge you to get a copy. Then read it and read it again until it becomes second nature in everything you do. That's what I a.m. doing.

William W
USA

FABULOUS!

Tom Poland gives you the science behind figuring out EXACTLY how to create demand and generate a flow of high-quality leads.

Buy this book and put the formula to work in your business — the results speak for themselves.

Dr Ivan Misner
Founder Business Network International (BNI) and *New York Times* best-selling author

ONE OF THE BEST BOOKS ON MARKETING EVER WRITTEN

Tom Poland is not only an expert marketer but a master teacher. Step- by-step instructions are easy to follow and you can build a complete marketing system without needing to be a genius. More practical and actionable than the 4-year marketing degree I completed.

Richard Petrie
Speed Marketing

SIMPLE TO READ AND EASY TO IMPLEMENT

When I read Tom Poland's last book, it was a treasure trove of knowledge and actionable advice.

And once again, he has delivered simple, easy-to-digest-and-implement content for me to grow my business.

When it comes to generating leads for your business, there are few people who will shoot you straight like Tom and give you the tools and roadmap to put them into play! Just get it and put this to work for yourself.

Brady S.
Canada

EASILY ONE OF THE MOST VALUABLE BUSINESS BOOKS I'VE READ

By this point I must have read over 400 books on marketing, sales, and business and I can honestly say I found this one of the most valuable.

So much useful stuff in Tom's book; it's accessible and Tom is a charming, down-to-earth guide, but the methodology is rigorous too. It's never dumbed down or over-simplified, because there is a lot to his lead-generation method.

Tom's model gives you not only a ton of useful ideas, but the overarching framework you need to fit them together. It's a complete system, and it gives you clarity.

Rob Tyson
The Tyson Report

A BOOK DEFINITELY WORTH BUYING

Business books that you don't want to put down are very rare, but Tom Poland's is one of them. He goes right to the heart of lead generation this wonderful book, which is full of real-world wisdom.

As the author of 47 books, I hate having to say that I wish I had written this one! It has certainly given me loads of ideas for improving my next book.

If I ever get the chance, I will invite Tom Poland to address my MBA students in one of the world's top business schools. They really need to know and understand material like this.

Professor Malcolm McDonald MA(Oxon) MSc PhD DLitt DSc
Emeritus Professor, Cranfield University School of Management
Author of *Marketing Plans* which sold over 500,000 copies

A HIGHLY ACTIONABLE BOOK THAT HELPS YOU CREATE A STRATEGY TO INCREASE LEADS INTO YOUR BUSINESS

I absolutely loved this book. Tom delivers so many practical tips for creating a lead generating machine. I highly recommend it to any business owner in need of leads!

Joshua Millage
Entrepreneur and co-founder of Lifter LMS

DON'T THINK ABOUT IT, GRAB THIS BOOK NOW AND BREAK DOWN THE BARRIERS HOLDING YOUR BUSINESS BACK!

Tom Poland's books are a great resource that lay out common marketing pitfalls. He then goes on to provide solutions to these challenges that slow people down from making the progress they desire to run a successful business -- ultimately enabling them to live an impactful life. The author's decades of experience are evident is his rich understanding of marketing, along with his insightful delivery. Don't think about it, grab this book now and break down the barriers holding your business back!

Charles Byrd
Evernote productivity guru

PUT THIS BOOK INTO PRACTICE THEN STEP BACK AND WATCH YOUR WHOLE WORLD CHANGE

In coaching business owners from start-up through $100M mark, I've seen more service-based companies waste more time, money, and energy on marketing than you would even believe. In SO many cases, it's all been a waste. This is particularly true for business owners who try to mimic info-marketing models.

The author explains not only why this doesn't work, but also how to evaluate your marketing efforts, explains how to properly define your ideal client, step-by-step instructions for crafting an effective message, advises on selecting the effective media, and a number of other critical topics.

If you read and implement what the author suggests in this book, you'll have done what 95% of marketers have NOT done; you'll have made your marketing as good as your service. And when that happens? Step back and watch your whole world change.

Robert Michon
The Unstoppable CEO

GREAT MARKETING BOOK FOR SERVICE PROFESSIONALS

This book is a tool chest of easy-to-use strategies to attract high numbers of high-quality clients.

Every chapter has some nuggets of wisdom that are easy to use. Highly recommended.

Graham McGregor
Marketing and sales consultant, trainer, coach

A MUST-READ BOOK

Brilliant! Tom Poland lays out a step-by-step process for creating a cut-through marketing message and then get that message out to the marketplace so that inbound new client enquiries flow in like turning on a tap.
As a successful consultant for over a decade, I recognize marketing gold when I see it.

Ari Galper
Author of *Unlock The Game*

PRACTICAL AND EFFECTIVE LEAD GENERATION SYSTEM

Practical, effective and implementable system that helps you create a predictable flow of high quality inbound new client inquiries into your business. Tom's book and system will show you how to stop random acts of marketing and get you back in the driver's seat running your business.

Susan Kleinschmidt
Consultant, trainer coach

AN INSIGHTFUL RESOURCE

Tom Poland offers a proven step-by-step lead-generation model – one that is beautifully tailored to his audience's specific needs. Grounded in professional experience and decades of observation, Tom writes with passion and deep knowledge.
An insightful, elegant, and practical resource – I certainly recommend it.

Dorie Clark
Marketing, branding and management consultant

COOL NEW LEAD GENERATION ROADMAP FOR SERVICE AND ADVISORY PROFESSIONALS

Not to toot my own horn, but I've been an internationally recognized expert on sales, lead generation and positioning for many years now, so I know a thing or two about great lead-generation systems.

There are tons of books out there on marketing, but what's different with Tom's books is that they are written for folks who specialize in service and/or advisory businesses, and not for those who sell physical products. They say that specificity is power, and I believe that the specific strategies in this book are what makes it so powerful. Tom's book truly "disrupts" the status quo and offers a road map that will lead you to generate a consistent flow of high quality, inbound leads.

Buy this book. Implement every suggestion. Then sit back and watch the new clients flow into your business.

Erik Luhrs
GURU Selling System

A TREASURE TROVE OF INFORMATION

A treasure trove of information not only about lead generation, but also about how to wire our whole business for success.

There are so many gems of information in this book, that if we even take one, and implement it, it makes a difference. I know that I've already changed my marketing message because of this, and people are much more interested in what I do now.

Glenda Nicholls
Founder, Money Success System

LEAD GENERATION: NOW A SIMPLE AND ELEGANT SCIENCE

Many of us employ a very hit and miss approach to marketing and lead generation – with very hit and miss results. Tom Poland however has turned lead generation into a science that is both simple and elegant.

In a market where we've all gotten used to the same old marketing formula, Tom brings a fresh approach that provides cut-through in a noisy world. You'll enjoy the easy-to-implement, step-by-step approach outlined in this book.

And, I have no doubt, you'll enjoy the results this unique system can generate.

Dawn Russell
Founder of Heartwired, trainer and coach

Contents

Preface

On March 23, 2020, the prime ministers of Singapore and Australia signed ten agreements to advance bilateral cooperation in new areas, including on data innovation and the digital economy.

Appropriately, given the theme of digital cooperation, the ceremony, including the signing of all agreements, was also completed not physically but virtually via videoconference and the use of touchscreen tablets complete with signatures from all parties using a handheld stylus, instead of the normal physical ink.

If this was not the first international agreement completed virtually, it was certainly one of the very earliest.

The reason the leaders of both countries met and concluded the agreement virtually was because of the global COVID-19 pandemic. The virtual signing ceremony was meant to have been a physical signing ceremony, but a world-wide lockdown made that unfeasible.

A physical meeting would have included the leaders of every relevant government department from Singapore, including the Prime Minister, complete with small teams of secretaries, security, ambassadors, caterers, medical staff, and more. They all would have flown in a large jet for eight hours, arrived in Canberra, Australia, and then the whole entourage would have been greeted at the airport with red carpets and a military guard ready for inspection. This would have been followed by banquets, dinner parties, meet-and-greets for all relevant dignitaries, and possibly off to the local zoo for a photo opportunity cuddling a koala and shaking hands with a kangaroo.

All of which proved to be completely unnecessary and simply an inefficient use of time, money, energy, and required the completely avoidable emission of hundreds of tons of greenhouse gases.

According to Ms Google, and she should probably know, virtual meetings became commercially viable in 2006. It's therefore taken 14 years and a global pandemic for governments to catch up to the potential of virtual meetings to replace the inefficiency of physical meetings.

But it's not just governments that have been slow to catch on to the massive efficiency improvements that virtual meetings offer; the commercial world has been equally as dismal in its failure to grasp the opportunity.

For example, I have a large network of highly-respected marketing colleagues and the vast majority of them have, up until the COVID-19 pandemic forced the complete shutdown of all conferences, seminars, workshops and trade shows, insisted that virtual meetings could never take the place of physical meetings. But just like the governments of Singapore and Australia, they have been forced to re-examine their beliefs.

NOT A ONE-OFF PHENOMENON

A paradigm is a belief through which we view reality. Psychologists tell us that paradigms change well after reality changes.

A classic and oft-mentioned example is that of Roger Bannister who, on May 6, 1954, was the first human in history to run a mile in less than four minutes. For the nine years prior to that, the world record stood at four minutes and 1.4 seconds. There's no question that many athletes viewed a sub-four-minute mile as a barrier that was beyond the limits of the human body. But just six weeks later, Australian John Landry ran even faster than Bannister and many others have followed in their footsteps.

The inability of world-class runners to break the four-minute mile until after the paradigm of impossibility was shattered is an example of how slow humans can be to challenge the limits of our perceptions and how we can be even slower to grasp an opportunity until we are faced with the stark reality of its potential.

Like most others, my mind is not smart enough nor fast enough to either challenge reality or to quickly jump on the potential that always arises when reality changes.

An exception occurred in 2008, when I just happened to be at the right time in my life and in the right circumstances, which included the luxury of being able to challenge the prevailing marketing paradigm that held that generating new clients in a premium-priced market necessitated the running of physical meetings in the form of free or paid seminars, workshops, trade shows, and conferences.

As a backgrounder, I had successfully launched, built, developed, and sold an international training business for entrepreneurs that had indeed necessitated the conducting of many such physical marketing events.

Having sold that business, however, I found myself happily unemployed and looking for my next business adventure.

I remember I was surfing the net, proactively looking for ideas when I came across a webpage that mentioned the word "webinar."

That really got my attention.

In the previous 13 years, I had run over 500 seminars and workshops that generated new clients and, although by other people's accounts, I was quite good at it, I was also "over it." I had enough of the flying, the driving, the traffic jams, the parking, the meet-and-greet prior to the seminars, and everything else that was involved in setting up and running an effective marketing event.

So I was intrigued.

What was this "webinar?"

Of course, like most digital innovations, this particular webinar was being held by two Americans and I was living in Australia. That meant I needed to get up at 3 a.m. to attend the webinar.

I still remember logging in, expecting to see two presenters on a stage talking to a virtual Audience a bit like I had been doing for the 13 previous years. Instead, what I got was "death by PowerPoint."

One presenter was droning on and on, while clicking through a series of slides and bullet point after boring bullet point. I guess they don't call them "bullet" points for nothing; this was a great way to kill off the Audience's interest.

I stuck around for the full hour hoping that it might get better.

It didn't.

A Good Idea in Shaky Hands

I can still recall quite clearly thinking to myself that, if that's a webinar, then they can stick it somewhere where the sun don't shine because I didn't want any part of it.

Nevertheless, I could see some potential if only the presentation style could be more engaging.

The next day, I became one of the early adopters of GoToWebinar by signing up for a subscription, a decision which has proved to be highly profitable for me.

Since 2008, I have conducted hundreds of webinars and generated millions of dollars in revenue.

In 2016, I began teaching other marketers how to do the same.

I consider myself to be genuinely blessed to have taught hundreds of clients in many industries across at least 19 times zones around the world how to generate new clients using webinars. And I love the richness that comes from the diversity of clients from different cultures and countries.

This book is a summary of my key learnings as a full-time professional engaged in marketing with webinars over the last 12 years, which includes teaching the science of marketing with webinars for the last four years.

It is my sincere wish that you will profit greatly from reading and implementing the information in this book. And should we choose to work together at some point, then I'm equally sincere in my desire for you to serve a greater number of your potential clients well beyond the borders of constraint that physical marketing events necessitate.

And in addition to being able to serve far greater numbers of your fellow human beings and generating significantly more revenue, the premium on this webinar cake is that the planet will thank you too, because running webinars is infinitely more environmentally friendly than running physical events.

Best, Tom Poland

Chief Leadsologist

www.Leadsology.Guru

www.MarketingWithWebinars.com

www.BookAChatWithTom.com

Introduction

THE NEW NORMAL FOR MARKETING VIA MEETINGS

PRIOR TO THE COVID-19 pandemic, the online meeting industry was growing steadily. But when the shutdowns hit, the number of subscriptions to online meeting platforms went through the stratosphere and you couldn't buy a decent Webcam for love nor money.

If we'd had a graph showing webinar usage, it would have run in tandem with the shocking graph lines tracking the explosive upswing in COVID-19 cases around the world.

Meanwhile, hundreds of millions of employees the world over were suddenly working from home, and the entire paradigm of needing to be physically together was shattered.

Many otherwise traditional businesses will continue to operate with the "new normal" of having remote workers on their teams, well and truly after COVID-19 has disappeared.

For now, as I type these words, every industry that involves the gathering of groups of people, including entertainment, travel, sports, and hospitality, is shut down. And that, of course, includes marketing events such as the multi-billion-dollar conference, seminar, and trade show industries.

Thankfully, they will all reopen once we have a vaccine for COVID-19, and at that point we will dispense with social-distancing measures.

But regardless of whether COVID-19 is still with us when you read this, I'd like to nominate the following points for your profitable consideration.

- **Profitability Point #1**: Until we have a vaccine for COVID-19, it would be profitable for you to develop the capability of generating new client inquires through webinars.

- **Profitability Point #2**: Post COVID-19, you can profit even more by keeping marketing webinars as an auxiliary revenue stream alongside whatever physical marketing events you are running. Webinars are a low-cost, simple, and when done my way (as opposed to "death by PowerPoint"), they are a highly profitable additional source of new client flows. I can't imagine why any growth-orientated person would not want that.

- **Profitability Point #3**: It is inevitable that scientists will succeed in developing a human vaccine for COVID-19. However, with over 100 other influenza viruses mutating and producing different strains every year, another epidemic or pandemic is equally inevitable. As Bill Gates loudly proclaimed for many years prior to COVID-19, it is only a question of when, not if. But on the subject of "if," what if in addition to a *human* vaccine, you had access to a *marketing* vaccine that would guarantee to keep your flow of new clients strong and healthy regardless of any pandemic? Marketing with webinars offers such a marketing vaccine that will eliminate the risk of any shutdown of new-client flows.

Regardless of your response to the above certainties, a new marketing normal of marketing with webinars is here to stay.

Of equal certainty is the fact that some of your competitors will develop the ability to generate additional new-client flows through webinars, and I'd therefore urge you to commit to developing the same capability before your competitiveness is eroded.

The final word on getting caught out without a webinar marketing alternative during a pandemic, goes appropriately to one of the world's most successful creators of stress and anxiety, author Stephen King:

"Fool me once, shame on you. Fool me twice, shame on me"

Carpe diem.

Chapter One:

Discover The Power Of Marketing With Webinars

How I Got Into Marketing With Webinars and Why I've Stuck With Them

I **mentioned in the** Preface how I stumbled across the idea of marketing with webinars in 2008 while looking to create my next business venture.

Previously, I'd organized myself as the main speaker for hundreds of physical events including seminars, workshops, and conferences because these events were such a great new-client generator for my business.

Understandably, many people who got to know me from my stage appearances made the mistake of assuming that I'm an extrovert which is a a bit like assuming a stand-up comedian is full of fun and laughter 24/7.

Nothing could be further from the truth. Sure, when I'm on stage and the spotlight is on me, my personality lights up like a Christmas tree and I love the thrill of engaging an entire Audience and having them laugh or bringing a tear to their eyes, all the while adding value and influencing their thinking in a significant and positive way.

All as a prelude to relieving them of some weight from their wallet, metaphorically speaking.

But truth be told, my default position for work is sitting right where I am at the moment, in front of a computer screen with Monty the Marketing Wonder Dog (Border Collie, thanks for asking) quietly snuffling in slumber at my feet as he recovers from our walk on the beach.

So the idea of being able to generate clients in every English-speaking country around the world while sitting in the comfort of my own home office and not having to travel anywhere and not having to pay conference centers hiring fees, and not having any parking hassles, and not having to actually talk with people physically fills my heart with great joy.

Do I still speak at conferences? Absolutely I do.

But I no longer organize them or risk my money promoting them or conducting them.

I simply show up and do what I do, which is to talk about marketing with webinars.

And I get paid to do that and I travel business class and stay in five class hotels and half the time my wife lets me carry her bags (translation: "she comes with me sometimes and we have a super-duper holiday after the conference").

So sure, I still speak at conferences, but when it comes to doing my own marketing, as I write these words, it's 100% through webinars.

Currently, I have clients in 27 cities and 17 time zones around the world. Since I cracked the webinar marketing code just a few short years ago, I figured out how to generate monthly revenue of more than six figures and with bigger, fatter profit margins than ever before.

ADVANTAGES OVER PHYSICAL SEMINARS

The explanation for why I continue to generate clients almost exclusively through webinars can be gleaned from the above, but I offer the following in the interests of elucidation:

7. When it comes to **a combination of efficiency and effectiveness,** there is literally no better medium on planet Earth for generating new clients, than a webinar.

8. Even for a one-person-act like my business, a webinar marketing system can **easily generate $100,000 or more of additional revenue every month with overheads of less than $200 a month.** Heck, a medium -sized enterprise should be able to add a million in revenue every month, and don't get me started on the potential for a larger organization.

9. A webinar can **reach Audiences in the building next door to you or Audiences on the other side of the world.** So long as the Audience understands your lan-

guage and has a half-decent internet connection, you can reach them with your offer.

10. Your **commute can be as short as mine:** from the espresso machine in your kitchen to a spare room at home. Your Audiences' commute can similarly be mercifully short.

11. One of my favorite benefits of marketing with webinars is the **incredibly short and explicitly direct link between a marketing action and a prospect's response**. You don't need any circuitous social media campaigns and you don't need any significant amount of patience because webinars give you enough time and space to establish yourself as your Audience members' number one supplier of choice.

12. There's an extremely high probability that if you were equipped with a powerfully persuasive webinar presentation that you knew would generate raving fans from the Audience as well as high-quality new-client inquiries, then **you would *want* to present** such a webinar. And the absence of that "want to" is, in my 39 years of marketing experience, why 97% of marketing efforts fail.

"Explain please Tom" I hear you ask.

OK...

Dogs want to bark, and cats want to meow.

Dogs should not try to meow, and cats should not try to bark.

What I'm saying here is that we all have *inclinations or preferences or desires* – call them what you will – that have us wanting to do certain things and not wanting to do certain other things.

If you're like me and your brain starts to hurt when viewing a five-year cash flow spreadsheet, there's a pretty good chance that you're a people-type person and not a numbers-type person.

If that's the case, then I urge you not to try and set up complicated online funnels which include split testing advertisements, ditto for landing pages, ditto for trip-wires, segmentation, and an analysis of at least seven metrics for each split test, pretty much every day that you're running an online final campaign.

I hope that you get this: ***If you don't want to do a thing, you will either never start it or you'll start and stop it, or you will do it badly.***

They are the only three possible outcomes.

Actually, truth be told, there is a fourth possible out-come, which is that you will force yourself, like a dog trying to meow, to do a thing that you don't want to do and you'll end up in a psychiatric ward because you bent yourself so far out of shape that you go nuts.

The bottom line here is that the absolute prerequisite for you getting a marketing method that works excep-tionally well is that you will want to do that thing, *OR* you have someone on your team who will want to do that thing.

And if you don't want to do it, then for the sake of your sanity as well as your bank account balance, find someone who does want to do that thing and you go ahead and stick to the thing that you were born to do and not the thing that someone else told you *should* do.

In the world of homo sapiens, *"want to"* gets done and *"should do"* doesn't get done.

In conclusion, when it comes to marketing and pretty much every other venture that you would like to be successful at in life, contrary to what your school-teachers or your parents may have taught you, success does not lie in discipline; it lies in focusing your energy and time and money on the things that you "want to" do and not on the things you are told you "should do."

13. Marketing with webinars gives you **the volume that you need minus the cost and complexity you don't want**. It would cost me $50,000 minimum to put 1,000 prospects into a conference center room, and I would have to start planning that event at least six months out. By contrast, I can put 1,000 prospects into a webinar with as little as six weeks' notice. And getting enough volume is critical to maximizing the profit from any event, offline or online.

To reinforce this point, consider this: in terms of results, the worst presentation in the world to one million prospects is going to beat the best presentation delivered to one prospect.

Volume fixes a multiple of deficiencies.

Better still, of course, is to fix those deficiencies *and* add volume. But nevertheless, if you don't have the volume, you've got nothing.

14. **Pre- and post-event notifications can be automated**. This includes sending advanced copies of the event playbook (notes outline) and reminders so you can "set and forget" that entire process.

Exactly the same is true for the event follow-up campaign.

If you follow the carefully-honed method I outline in Chapter Five, you'll not only maximize your attendance rates at every webinar, but you'll also double your results from the webinar with an automated follow-up sequence.

Note well: A lot of webinar presenters boast they double their webinar results by offering a replay after the live webinar; however, they also drop their attendance rates by as much as 80% by offering a replay. And according to my math, doubling 20% is a hell of a lot less than doubling 100%. See Chapter Five for more.

WHICH PRODUCTS AND SERVICES CAN BE MARKETED WITH WEBINARS?

I was going to list each of the 197 industries for which I've generated leads, but that would fill too much of this book and I want to save every page for information that is more valuable to you so let me just say this:

Marketing with webinars can generate leads for any product, any service, at any price point, to any market.

One of the banes of my existence is hearing people say something like: "I can see that marketing with webinars would work well for you, but I don't think it'll work well for me because [fill in the excuse here].

The "because" is followed by the speaker's personalized million-dollar-losing disqualifier that comes in the form of "my product is different" or "my market is different" or "I am in a big city and you live at the beach," or "I'm a vegan and you're a meat eater," or "my country is different," or "I don't have fiber optic Internet cable," or "my price point is different," or "my Audiences don't attend webinars" (unless your Audience is dead people, this is absolute B.S.), or whatever other reason their unconscious mind comes up with that prevents them from seeing their bank account fill with hundreds of thousands of dollars.

There isn't a microscope that's been made yet that can examine what the heck it is that goes on in someone's unconscious mind. So, until that's been invented, we just have to guess.

And my guess is that people come up with these disqualifiers because marketing with webinars takes away one of the last remaining excuses to step up and be responsible for generating results that would make them a superstar.

Why would the unconscious prevent them from seizing the opportunity?

Simple: It's the same reason that demotivates the vast majority of underachievers — the fear of disappointment.

If they don't try something, they can't fail.

If they can't fail, then they can't experience disappointment.

The unconscious will go to the ordinary lengths to protect a human being from feeling something they don't want to feel.

My strongest recommendation is that as soon as you notice your unconscious coming up with reasons for why marketing with webinars won't generate millions in revenue for your organization, immediately redirect it to come up with reasons why marketing with webinars will generate millions, regardless of your product / service / market / country / price / gender / etc.

The final word goes to the late, great Dudley Houghton, my first business mentor:

"The most expensive thing we can ever own is a closed mind."

CHAPTER TWO:

How to Fill Your Webinars With High-quality Audiences

AT A STRATEGIC level, marketing is actually very simple. You need three things.

You need to have something that makes a difference in people's lives or businesses and I call that something your magic.

Then you need to message that magic in such a way that, when it's in front of your market, people notice it and are motivated to want to know more or to buy.

My very simple marketing model is therefore this:

*You need an **Audience** made up of your target market, an **Asset** through which you can get the message about your magic to that market and, then you need a Call to **Action** so your **Audience** knows how to buy or inquire.*

This chapter deals with where you find your Audiences.

The following chapters will deal with the other two elements, being the Asset (which in the context of webinars is your presentation), and your Call to Action of which there are two main types —an offer for a prospect to meet and talk about your product/service, or to go ahead and buy.

More on that soon.

In the meantime, the most important thing I can tell you about finding Audiences is that the source of your Audience is the number one determinant of your success in marketing with webinars.

Think about it like this: I mentioned that I had the good fortune to live in a home which sits literally on the white sand next to the sea at little Castaways Beach in sub-tropical Queensland, Australia.

And if that's not heavenly enough, our house sits on a large block of land next to a park including trees with clinging koalas, kickboxing kangaroos, and kleptomaniac kookaburras (yes, our feathered friends will steal a sandwich as you raise it from your plate to your mouth, I kid you not!).

Amongst which is also my private collection of Australian stingless bees sitting in four hives under the shade of our Eucalyptus trees and bamboo.

To complete the picture, you need to also imagine my dog's dinner bowl which sits outside our back door.

To illustrate the point that where you get your Audiences from is critical, imagine that on the kitchen bench in our house, I have two items: the first is a nice juicy red steak and the second is a beautiful bouquet of flowers.

Now imagine me calling Monty the Marketing Wonder Dog for dinner and opening the door to allow him to enthusiastically bound outside complete with tail wagging, teeth grinning, and mouth drooling in anticipation of the steak that he can no doubt smell.

Now further imagine the look on my furry friend's face when I place the bouquet of flowers in his dinner bowl. Needless to say, he is going to look at me with those puppy dog eyes, tilting his head as he does so, in the canine personification of puzzlement.

Equally puzzled would be the bees should I place a steak in front of the beehive, although their tiny little frowns would be harder to see, I'll grant you that.

The bees won't be biting into the steak, any more than Monty will be munching on the flowers.

But switch the steak with the flowers, and the response would be electric.

All of which is to say that if you get the wrong Audience on your webinars, it's going to be as hard to get them buying as it is to get my dog to eat the flowers.

And it's not just a matter of finding an Audience that is a *fit* for your product or service; it's also a matter of selecting the best *quality* Audience for your offer.

The last time I counted, there were 115 different sources of Audiences, but not all sources are created equal.

I'm not a fan of the idea, but indeed it's possible to make money by accessing an Audience from a cold-calling source or from a cold-email source, provided your methodology is sophisticated enough and you are prepared to go through a large volume of "suspects" in order to find a qualified prospect.

Once again, in the interests of providing value and not filler, I'll skip listing every single Audience source and highlight several which are worthwhile and one which towers above every other source in terms of a combination of quality, cost, and longevity.

SEO

Search Engine Optimization is the process of growing the quality and quantity of website traffic by increasing the visibility of your website to users of a web search engine, which these days typically means Google.

SEO does not involve direct advertising costs, but rather relies on carefully curated content that is aligned with the search rules which Google, in its infinite wisdom, chooses to change every year or so.

In general terms, SEO starts with figuring out what keyword phrases your ideal clients are typing in when using Google to find information about your type of product or service.

If you go to Google right now and type in the phrase "inbound marketing book," then it's likely that my last bestseller by the same name will appear in the top four search results, assuming you scroll down underneath the paid advertisements. Look for the bright yellow cover and thank you in advance for your contribution to next month's royalty check.

Before I wrote that book, I had someone much smarter than I am who is a specialist in getting found on Google do the research and figure out that people were searching for that phrase.

Effective marketing is simple: it creates an offer that you know people already are looking for.

Effective marketing does not try and convince people that they should buy what you've got.

That's what effective selling does.

Selling is what you have to do when your marketing sucks.

And if you are a marketer, before you get too smug, let me tell you that *marketing* is what you have to do when your *selling* sucks.

It's just that I happen to prefer the magic of marketing over the magic of selling and I still defer to the age-old wisdom that says, *"a person convinced against their will is a person who remains unconvinced."*

In other words, the better you are at selling, the more prospects you will convert to clients, but that will probably extrapolate into clients who don't stay around very long.

Back to the point at hand, however, which is that SEO can deliver a steady stream of registrants for your webinar. If you're interested in that (and why wouldn't you be?), then I'm not your guy. I'm the webinar expert and my specialty is getting Audiences without cost or complication (see OPN below).

So if you want SEO help, find an SEO expert just like I did.

I will caution, however: developing an SEO strategy to fill your Audiences is not simple and neither is it easy or fast. Plus it will cost you a fair bit of money.

That's the bad news with SEO.

The good news is that, once you do get it right, it can deliver prospects to your webinars for years to come.

So, it's worth exploring but I would not recommend it as your first strategy for finding Audiences for your webinar. But it is one that's definitely worthy of consideration after you've successfully implemented my OPN strategy.

PPC

This stands for Pay Per Click and again I am not an expert on this method. Like SEO, I have previously consulted with clients in this area, but as this marketing method has evolved, it requires a level of experience and sophistication that I simply can't keep up with.

PPC is an Internet advertising model used to drive traffic to websites and webinars in which you as the advertiser pay a publisher when the advertisement is clicked. That publisher is typically a search engine such as Google, or website owner, or a network of websites. More specifically, examples include Google ads, Amazon advertising, and Microsoft advertising, which was formally known as Bing Ads. Social networks such as Facebook, LinkedIn, Pinterest, Twitter, Instagram, and TikTok, as well as YouTube, also offer advertising services.

Whatever we call it and whichever platform you choose to advertise on, PPC starts with the same first step as SEO, which is to lure people wanting more information about your type of product or service. Bearing in mind that, depending on the size of your company and your brand's "share of mind," it's unlikely that they'll be searching directly for your name or your product or service's name.

And just like SEO, PPC can deliver significantly profitable results when it's done right. But again, just like SEO, getting results can take quite a bit of time and a fair old chunk of change, which is why I don't recommend that you start trying to generate Audiences from PPC, but rather through my OPN strategy which I'll detail shortly.

AFFILIATES

Affiliate marketing is now a multibillion-dollar industry in its own right.

It's a type of performance-based marketing in which a business rewards one or more affiliates for each visitor or customer brought in by the affiliate's own marketing efforts.

Typically, a commission is paid from each sale for each customer introduced by the affiliate marketer, and in my game, affiliates are often used to drive registrants to a webinar.

The benefit of affiliate marketing to the owner of the product or service being sold is that you don't pay for a sale until after it's been made. You simply take a percentage of the sale price from the revenue paid to you by the new customer, and you put that percentage into the bank account of the affiliate. So you only pay after you've been paid and that's a tremendous advantage over any form of advertising where you pay before you get paid, *if* you get paid at all.

The disadvantage of affiliate marketing is that, unlike SEO or PPC, a professional affiliate will want to see some evidence of how well your product sells before they'll devote their time, energy, and often significant resource to generating buyers for your service or product.

They will want to know, for example, how many people buy out of every hundred who visit your website sales page, or who register for your webinar.

And they will want to know what the average transaction size is.

Depending on the nature of the product or service that you're selling, they will want anything between 20% and 50% of the sale price, so you need to make sure you've got very healthy profit margins before you engage in affiliate marketing.

As mentioned above, affiliate marketing generates billions of dollars in revenue every year and it's getting bigger every year, but unless you have all your marketing metrics clearly established, it's not the place to start. You need to prove to a professional affiliate marketer that you can convert traffic from suspects to prospects to buyers. Start by getting your Audiences from OPN and then add Audiences from LinkedIn using the methods I outline below.

LinkedIn

When it comes to a quality source of Audiences, LinkedIn is one of the best.

But it doesn't work optimally the way most LinkedIn marketing experts tell you that it works.

Note well: I'm not saying that LinkedIn doesn't work the way that most experts tell you that it works, but rather I'm saying it doesn't work *best* that way.

Most LinkedIn marketing experts will tell you that the first step in every successful LinkedIn campaign is to carefully identify "suspects." I call them suspects because during this first step we can only *suspect* that they might be a prospect.

I agree wholeheartedly that the very first step of any successful LinkedIn campaign is going to be compiling a list of LinkedIn members who fit the profile of your ideal client.

(This book is not about marketing 101, so if you want more on how to identify an ideal client, then you should grab a copy of *Leadsology® The Science of Being In Demand*.)

Where other LinkedIn marketing experts and I part company is at the next step.

What you've probably heard is that having created a list or a group of your ideal client suspects, you then send them a series of 12 or 19 or 99 (the numbers vary depending on which expert you listen to) added-value, content-rich messages or posts over a 90-day period.

Some experts suggest that you can automate this process and others say you should do it manually. It doesn't really matter how you do it because it's not going to work particularly well either way.

It took me a lot of time and a lot of effort and a fair chunk of money to figure this out, so you would do well to pay careful attention to the follow statement:

LinkedIn does not work best (key word) using a content rich, nurture style, marketing method.

By contrast, the nurture-with-quality-content method works well for someone coming to your website and opting in for some free content, be that a white paper, or a checklist, or a mind map, or whatever.

But nurture-with-quality-content doesn't work so well for LinkedIn connections.

The reason is to be found in the difference in prioritization of interests between an email subscriber and a LinkedIn connection.

An email subscriber's first priority of interest is the benefit of your product or service and secondly to confirm that you are a supplier who is professional and reliable and easy to deal with.

At the risk of repeating myself (but this is an important point), when it comes to visitors subscribing with their email address on your website, no one is interested in **you** until after they have established their interest in the benefit of your service or product.

With LinkedIn, however, the order of their priority of interest is reversed.

First and foremost, they are interested in you and then, and only then, do you have even the faint possibility that they might be interested in the benefit of your product or service.

The reason that LinkedIn connections are mostly interested in you first and foremost, comes down to context, or more specifically, down to the nature of the medium.

LinkedIn is a business network.

People join up because they want to connect with prospects.

And you can divide prospects into two broad categories within LinkedIn: the recruitment category and the selling category.

In the recruitment category, you'll find recruitment professionals who are looking to head-hunt talent for their clients. Also in this category are the executives who have sharpened up their profile to attract the headhunters so they might receive a better offer for employment than what they're currently enjoying, or not enjoying, as the case may be.

But whether they are the headhunter or the headhuntee, they still fit into the category of recruitment.

In the category of the sellers, you'll also find two subcategories.

The first are hoping to sell you their product or service and the second subcategory are those hoping to sell their products or services to your network.

Please note that there is no third category of people who wake up in the morning and think "oh goody I'll log in to my LinkedIn account and if I'm lucky someone will sell me something."

The category of "people looking to buy stuff" belongs to the Amazon store or the eBay store or to any other online store. LinkedIn is not an online store. A different context requires a different strategy.

So, let's forget the recruitment category and focus on the balance, which is the people who are hoping to sell something to someone.

The prioritization of their interest is therefore **you**, first and foremost. Not your product or service.

Therefore, the very best method for generating leads from LinkedIn is what I call "connect invite."

You find people who you suspect may become ideal clients and you connect with them.

As soon as the connection request is accepted you invite them to your webinar.

In Chapter Six, you'll be able to explore "Boardroom Briefings" which is a type of webinar that I typically invite LinkedIn connections to attend. Until Chapter Six, it's enough for you to be aware of the following numbers.

Depending on your industry, it's most likely that between 30% and 33% will accept your connection request. That's because, according to LinkedIn itself, that's the percentage of their members who are active on LinkedIn at least more than once a month.

When you receive a connection request and you give that person the invitation to join you on your webinar, 2.5% will register to attend.

Provided that registrant is reminded and encouraged to honor their registration, up to 70% of that 2.5% which came from the 33%, will attend your webinar.

And depending on the product and service and the way you structure the Call to Action at the end of your webinar (more on that in Chapter Five), 25% of attendees will become clients.

If you work the math backwards from how many new clients you want, then you can figure out how many connection requests you need to make.

But regardless of how many new clients you want, I can assure you that you will need to make a bucketload of connection requests.

I don't know about you, but the last thing I want to fill my life with is connecting with hundreds of LinkedIn members and inviting him to attend my webinar every week.

If you feel the same, then you've got two options. You can automate the connection and invitation process. Or you can hire freelancers to connect with LinkedIn members and to invite those people to your webinar, on your behalf.

LinkedIn most certainly has a pathologically destructive dislike of automated connection platforms. If they so much as get a whiff that you are using such a platform, they will suspend your membership.

I've used various platforms over the years and naturally some are better than others, but they all have one inherent weakness, which is that they don't possess (at least at the time of this writing) any form of reasonably sophisticated artificial intelligence.

That means they're not capable of responding to the random and unpredictable questions from some of the very best prospects. By the way, the very best prospects are often the ones who ask questions, and by setting up some sort of irrelevant but automated response, you can kill off their interest very quickly.

So, the best solution is neither for you to be wasting endless hours connecting and inviting suspects, nor is it to automate the process.

I teach my clients to do exactly what I do, which is to find high-quality LinkedIn specialist freelancers and buy five hours of their time every week, paying them a retainer of five dollars an hour along with a $50 bonus for every LinkedIn member who attends my webinar.

Of course, the terms of remuneration will change from time to time, but at the time of this writing that's what they are.

My favorite source of LinkedIn specialists is **www.upwork. com** and my favorite country to source them from is Bangladesh. Mostly, their English is good enough to respond to the inevitable questions that are asked by some of the better-quality prospects which they'll be engaging with.

In summary, LinkedIn is undoubtably one of the best sources of prospects and even more so if you're targeting time-poor and stressed senior executives, and/or if you have a relatively high-priced product or service.

But regardless of whether that's the case, the source of prospects that beats every other single source on the planet is OPN.

OPN

Overview

OPN stands for Other Peoples' Networks and a basic premise here is that, regardless of your target market, someone else is targeting it.

And I'm not talking about your competitors.

Mostly, I'm referring to people or organizations that want to sell into the same market as you, but who offer a different product or service.

Some people call this method "host beneficiary" and others call it "joint venture," but I deliberately avoid using those terms because there are differences to my method and it's easier for me to communicate effectively how OPN works if I can empty my Audience's minds of what they think I'm talking about, before I begin explaining.

Many years ago, I took my three young daughters to their Saturday morning sports ground.

On parking the car, they scattered to three different corners of the sports ground and each played their little hearts out and gave the best for their team. I skipped from one field of play to the next rooting for them, one by one.

On this particular morning, by the time I rounded them up, they each had in their little hot hands a voucher which entitled the bearer of said voucher to one free hamburger from McDonald's for every five gallons of gas purchased at a Shell service station bowser.

Needless to say, I had little option but to stop at the nearest Shell service station, no matter that it was many miles out of our way, and fill up my tank with 15 gallons of gas.

I was then ordered by my three little Panzer tanks in skirts to drive to the nearest McDonald's drive-through to redeem the three free hamburgers.

And what do you think my chances were of getting away with ordering just the three free hamburgers?

Correct: a big fat zero.

Three lots of fries, three lots of Coke and three chocolate ice cream sundaes later, I pulled out of that drive-through with a wallet that was significantly lighter, having redeemed our "free" hamburgers.

God bless McDonald's, right?

And I remember thinking "what just happened here?"

And then of course, I connected the dots.

Shell and McDonald's combined to create the mother of all OPNs by sprinkling those darned vouchers around every sports center across our fair city, like confetti at a wedding.

Having thus illustrated the power of OPN, let me drill down on the three reasons why I've consistently used this one method as my primary source for generating new clients, since 1995.

Reason number one: OPN generates new clients for free.

And I find that to be a very good price indeed.

Reason number two: OPN is a source of new clients that is completely inexhaustible.

There's no point in fishing a pond dry because then you're going to go hungry, but with OPN the resource is 100% sustainable. You can "rinse and repeat" my OPN method for the rest of your lifetime and another hundred lifetimes to come and you still won't have overfished the resource.

Reason number three: OPN is the best quality source of prospects bar none*.

(*That is, outside of unsolicited client referrals, which you have no direct control over.)

As you read the following pages, I invite you to see how those three reasons stack up.

Having worked this methodology for 25 years and counting, I have yet to find a source of new clients that is free, inexhaustible, and of very high quality.

On countless occasions, I have invited Audiences, including Audiences full of marketing specialists, to contact me urgently should they discover a better source of clients than OPN.

I'm still waiting.

In broad terms, OPN consists of (1) identifying and (2) qualifying a person or an organization who has an email list, within which reside your prospective ideal clients.

That person or key stakeholder within that organization is (3) approached with an offer that you know they are already looking for.

They then (4) engage with you and you (5) convert them from a prospect into an OPN Partner. You then both engage in a cross-marketing campaign to each other's Audiences, just like Shell and McDonald's did in my example above, and proceed to (6) maximize your relationship through the process of debriefing and referral to other partners who are also proven reliable cross-marketers.

I have a "Plan A" and a "Plan B" for my OPN Partners and, in the interest of shedding further light on this wonderful opportunity, let me just say that Plan A involves me presenting a live webinar to the other organization's email subscriber list, and vice versa.

Plan B involves the other organization promoting some form of my other static (versus "live") content, such as a free download in the form of a checklist, or blueprint, or an e-book or similar, and vice versa.

As you can see, OPN is a reciprocal cross-marketing method.

The following drills down a little deeper on each of the six OPN steps mentioned above.

OPN Step 1: Identification

This is the easy part.

Simply open up your browser to your favorite search-engine page which is probably Google, type in a phrase that describes your target market, and then type in any one of a number of marketing mediums.

For example, if you're a business coach and you said the small business market you could type in "small business" as the descriptive of your target market and then you could type in either "webinar" or "seminar" or "book" or "e-book" or "podcast" or "blog" or any number of other marketing mediums.

The list produced by your search engine will probably include hundreds of thousands, if not a million or more potential OPN Partners.

Identification is really that easy.

But, of course, it's nowhere near enough.

All you've got now is a list of suspects and we have to take the next step to turn them into qualified OPN Prospects.

OPN Step 2: Qualification

THE FIVE KNOCK-OUT FACTORS

In New Zealand, there is an extinct bird called the Moa.

Apparently, it looked a bit like a giant emu and early explorers heard rumors of this great bird from the indigenous Maori, who had previously enjoyed eating it because it was pretty much the only decent sized animal in the country.

(Apparently you can only eat so many little bony Kiwis before you get tempted to go for the "up-size me" offer.)

Unfortunately, the Maori were such great hunters and had such a healthy appetite that it was thought that they had hunted the bird to extinction.

However, in the early years of settlement, rumors persisted of Moa sightings, but they proved about as reliable as sightings of the Loch Ness monster or the Abominable Snowman.

Nevertheless, it didn't stop a lot of expeditions exploring some of the mountainous and most heavily forested areas in New Zealand in search of the elusive Moa.

Alas, to no avail.

As a well-known New Zealand song laments, *"They're gone and they ain't no Moa."*

The reason I'm sharing this bit of trivia with you is that if you are going to go hunting for a Moa, then you better at least first know what they look like.

And it's the same deal with a prospective OPN Partner: you need to figure out what your ideal OPN Partner looks like before you go hunting for them.

Unfortunately, because of the broad range of my intended readership, it's not possible for me to give everyone a detailed checklist of what to look for in an OPN Partner. But I can give you the key characteristics that will apply to pretty much every single industry segment on our planet.

I recommend that you take the following key characteristics and draft your own Ideal OPN Partner Checklist, and once you have been able to identify and engage successfully with a series of OPN Partners, you'll be able to create a more refined checklist. At that point, you can outsource this step to a smart freelancer who will go hunting for your Moas.

1. The first characteristic is that your prospective OPN Partners should be targeting the same target market as you.

For example, my prospective OPN Partners target business owners and executives who are interested in sales and marketing.

2. The second characteristic is that, if you are offering a service, they should be offering a service; or if you are offering a physical product, they also should offer a physical product.

Don't try and conduct any form of cross-marketing campaign with someone who is offering a product if you are offering a service. The same applies if you are offering a product and someone else is offering a service.

For example, if I attempted an OPN campaign with a computer supply company, it would fail dismally. Their Audience is conditioned to receiving offers for physical products, not for professional services such as mine.

Don't ask me why, but it just flat out doesn't work if an email list that has been built on the back of physical products is offered professional services. And vice versa.

3. The third characteristic is they need to be actively marketing.

Effective marketing puts an offer in front of someone who is already looking for that offer.

Never try and convince a prospective OPN Partner that conducting a cross-marketing campaign is a good idea.

Sure, even a blind squirrel will find an acorn in a forest once in a while, but I recommend that you pursue a strategy where the likelihood of your success is 90% as opposed to a 10% likelihood, which is what you have when you try to convince someone to change their strategy or to adopt your strategy.

It's easy to tell if a person or an old organization is actively marketing. Just ask Ms Google to search their name, and if they have a significant web presence (not just a significant website) then they are a prospect.

4. The fourth characteristic is they have at least one email opt-in on their website.

The chances of an individual or an organization having a great email list without any email opt-in on their website ranks right up there alongside the chances of the blind squirrel enjoying a satisfying meal. It's possible, but not probable, so let's stick to playing the odds.

5. The fifth characteristic is that they have engaged in the marketing medium that you have prepared and are ready to go.

I mentioned above that my Plan A is to conduct a cross-promotion of each other's webinars. Therefore,

I want to make sure that my prospective OPN Partner is already running webinars.

If that's the case, then I know it's extremely likely that my offer of providing an Audience is something that they would grab in a heartbeat.

Likewise, if I wanted someone to promote my book, I'd be approaching someone who has a book that they would like to promote.

The above are what I call the Five Knockout Factors. If a prospect fails to tick <u>all</u> five characteristics, then they are no longer a prospect.

It took me eleven years to develop the Five Knockout Factors.

Prior to the Five Knockout Factors, I had success with approximately one out of every ten prospective OPN Partners I approached.

After I applied the Five Knockout Factors, that changed to one successful OPN campaign for every four OPN Prospects identified.

By the way, that's 11 years of testing in my capacity as a full-time professional marketer. And I'm handing my findings to you for the price of a book.

So please, don't think, not even for a moment, that the Five Knockout Factors are of only passing interest. They represent the opportunity to build a multi-million dollar distribution channel, without any significant cost or complication.

As mentioned, The Five Knockout Factors gave me a one-in-four success rate, but I took that to three in four with the next qualification method.

JV Juice

Every marketing method has its benefit and its cost.

To figure out if any particular method is worthwhile, you have to consider not just the benefit but also the cost. The difference between the two is what you base your decisions on.

If a paid advertising campaign brings you $1,000,000 and it costs you $100,000, then that strategy stacks up pretty well.

By contrast, if you spend a thousand hours on LinkedIn and come up with one prospect who doesn't buy, than the cost-benefit ratio is not so great.

My OPN strategy is no different: you need to weigh up the cost with the benefit.

Hopefully, I've already impressed upon you that the benefit is significant.

And the good news is that there is no financial cost to generating new client flows from OPN, but there is a different form of cost, which is the days you need to dedicate to marketing your OPN Partner's offer in your marketing calendar.

Every time I promote an OPN partner's webinar, in exchange for them promoting my webinar, I use up a chunk of my marketing calendar. Typically, that promotion is conducted over five days.

One email invitation goes out to my email subscribers five days prior to their webinar presentation, and another one goes out two days prior.

That's the thick end of a whole week used up in my marketing calendar to promote someone else's webinar.

And that's absolutely fine, and it's a very worthwhile use of my marketing calendar unless my OPN Partner turns out to be a dud.

At the time of this writing, the "sweet spot" for me is an OPN partner who can generate 100 to 200 registrants. That's because I can reciprocate at that level when promoting their webinar to my list.

Approximate reciprocation is the key to a successful OPN Partnership.

That means that it's no good for me to approach someone who can get me a million webinar registrants because I can't come close to reciprocating at that level, at least not at the time of writing these words.

Likewise, I don't want to approach someone who can only get me eight registrants because that's not reciprocating at my level either, because selecting a dud OPN Partner can easily cost me $25,000 of revenue.

That's expensive because it chews up a week of my marketing calendar that could have used for a more suitable OPN Partner.

So, after I developed The Five Knockout Factors, my mind turned to how I could improve on my one in four OPN Prospect success ratio.

To cut a very long story short, I hired a couple of data scientists (yes, such people exist, complete with PhDs) to figure out if we could use information that can be scraped from a prospective OPN partners website and use those metrics to provide a prediction of how many registrants the owner of that website would likely generate for my webinar.

Theses super-smart dudes started by examining the full range of 155 OPN Partners who had promoted my webinars up until that date. They worked backwards from the results of all those webinar promotions and matched those numbers with metrics from the OPN Partners' websites.

To be clear: they were looking for a correlation between the number of webinar registrants generated by each OPN Partner and the metrics that we could legally scrape from each OPN Partner's website.

I fully admit that when I began the Registrant Prediction Algorithm Project, as I lovingly christened it, I felt like Don Quixote tilting at windmills.

I didn't have a lot of faith in the likely success of the project.

And in the early weeks, it felt like we were simply stabbing in the digital darkness.

But fifteen months and a whole lot of cash later, my data scientists have developed an algorithm that accurately predicts how many registrants a prospective OPN partner is likely to generate for my webinar, prior to us approaching that person.

When I share the algorithm with my marketing colleagues, they are at first understandably skeptical. And then when they see the algorithm demonstrated, they are astonished.

Update for your information: "Registrant Prediction Algorithm" describes the platform very well, but it's not a particularly sexy marketing name so I have rechristened it "JV Juice" (Joint Venture Juice) and you can take it for a free test drive here: **www.JVjuice.com**

Also, JV Juice works well for any form of OPN/JV Partnership where you want to know in advance how many email opt-ins a person or an organization is likely to generate for you whether your offer is an e-book (e.g. **https://www.leadsology.guru/inboundmarketingbook**) or something like a five-day challenge (e.g. **www.FiveHourChallenge.com**) or indeed, a webinar (e.g. **www.LeadGenDemo.com**).

JV Juice is as close to a marketing miracle as I've ever seen because it's like having your own crystal ball that predicts the likely success of engaging with any OPN Partner before you approach them. And *"before"* is the key word here.

Since JV Juice, my revenue is up because I'm batting close to four-out-of-four successes with my OPN Partners, thanks to the Five Knock Out factors and JV Juice, both of which you can also benefit from without fee due to the fact that I've given you the former and that I offer a "freemium" version of the latter.

When I explained to a marketing colleague that JV Juice qualifies prospective partners so I can find those who can generate Audiences for my webinars that are not too small and not too big – my "sweet spot," as I referred to it above – he said "Wow, so it's like Tinder for JVs... swipe left for no, swipe right for yes!."

And I guess he's right.

OPN Step 3: Approach

Let's assume that you followed the above two steps and that you've identified and qualified an ideal OPN Partner.

One of the big mistakes that almost everyone who is new to marketing makes is thinking that most of the hard work has been done in identifying and qualifying a prospect.

When it comes to OPN, or for that matter any form of joint venture marketing, simply approaching the prospect with something like *"boy, have I got a deal for you"* is going to end in tears.

Your tears. Not theirs.

Because you won't even hear back from them.

Not unless they are desperate, and you really don't want to be doing deals with desperate people.

This is where a little bit of patience will go a long way.

Rather than approaching your newly identified and well-qualified OPN Prospect with the offer for some sort of reciprocal marketing campaign, you'll have a lot more success by offering something that's going to provide them with significant value but much less risk.

Something they are already looking for.

But, you may ask, why would they sense risk?

Because they don't know you from a bar of soap. And humans are sensibly hard-wired to associate the unknown with risk. It's why we still exist as a species, despite our best efforts to kill each other off with epidemics, climate change, and nuclear weapons.

And that's what this step, the approach, is all about: making them an offer that's super-low in perceived risk but high in perceived value. An offer that's too good for them to say "no" to.

My main approach strategy is to invite them onto my podcast.

Our approach email takes them to my podcast showcase webpage which, please forgive me, but I won't reveal here because we're quite selective about who we invite onto the podcast.

(Email **support@leadsology.guru** to see if you may be a fit. Thanks for understanding.)

The thing about inviting a guest onto my podcast is that I'm providing them with a platform to get their message out to their target market, many of whom happen to be sitting in my email subscriber list.

I know that's the case because of the preceding two steps: identification and qualification.

By the way, keep reading because, just in case you don't have an email list at the moment, I'll show you how to grow one very quickly, which is also of high quality. So, don't disqualify yourself from this strategy simply because you don't have an email list right now.

Having identified and qualified my OPN Prospect, now I'll approach them with an offer that's easy for them to say "yes" to, because it offers them a tangible benefit with minimum risk.

OPN Step 4: Engage

This is not to say that every podcast guest is someone that I want to conduct an OPN campaign with. There are guests that I want to have on my show simply because they have a great message and can add a lot of value to my email subscribers.

My email subscribers are the most valuable asset I have in my business.

I want to look after them and make sure they stay subscribed by giving them quality content both in the form of podcast episodes as well as the webinars presented by my OPN Partners.

Having said that, virtually every OPN partner is firstly a podcast guest.

That's because I can establish the four levels of what I call Psychological Allure, in under 30 minutes.

The four levels include Rapport (our personalities click), Respect (for my professionalism and reliability), Relatability (to my Audience and my offer) as well as the most powerful marketing psychology of all which is Reciprocity.

The latter being Homo Sapiens' unconscious compulsion to want to keep the "giving score" approximately even. I do something cool for you, then all other things being equal, you'll want to do something cool for me.

If you propose an OPN campaign to your prospect *before* you have established those four levels of Psychological Allure, then you're probably fail. Trust me on that; before I figured out the Reciprocity bit, I did a lot of failing.

If you skipped step 4 (Engage), it would be like proposing marriage the first time you saw someone. And we really didn't need the reality TV show "Married At First Sight" to realize that rarely ends well.

OPN Step 5: Convert

This is where the Godfather Strategy comes in.

Once you've established the Four Levels of Psychological Allure, then it's time to make the offer of an OPN Partnership.

I don't recommend, however, that you come out with any specific offer at this point. Rather, simply dangle the carrot of exploring the potential of an OPN arrangement in general terms.

Of course, if you've done your homework and you've properly identified and qualified and engaged your prospect, then converting them from a prospect into a partner should really be a slam dunk.

As simple and as smooth as a hot knife through soft butter because the hard work has already been done. The lid has already been loosened.

The people who come unstuck are the ones who rush this process and go from identification, skip qualification, go straight to approach, and if by some miracle they get a response, they then skip engagement, and go straight for the conversion offer.

And they fail.

And they fail, time after time.

And they wonder how come others are making OPN work.

There are no shortcuts: you have to move through every step, one at a time, in order to maximize the profits in OPN.

But even though there are not shortcuts, my system gives you a faster and surer route.

And with the next step, an infinitely more profitable route.

OPN Step 6: Maximize

Maximization is where most of the money is to be made in any OPN Partnership.

Once you complete a successful OPN campaign, you then need to debrief and confirm that each party was able to reciprocate at a level that the other was happy with.

If that's not the case, then one party needs to make it up, maybe with an additional promotion, so that both parties walk away from the campaign happy that they were involved.

Once reciprocation is confirmed, then it's time to refer each other to other OPN Partners who you each know to be proven and successful at the same level that you were able to reciprocate at.

A failure to cross-refer is the reason why most of the gold remains buried for most people who conduct any form of cross-marketing campaign.

I'll bet you Shell and McDonald's had a debrief and if their representatives were smart, they would have asked for introductions to other proven successful OPN Partners.

How to Organize Your Marketing Calendar for Maximum Results

You read above about how my marketing calendar becomes a bottleneck.

So I wanted to take a little space here and explain the concept of a marketing calendar in case you're unfamiliar with the notion.

A marketing calendar is simply a normal calendar where you schedule your marketing events, including social media posts, podcast releases, and running events such as webinars.

But first, note that the purpose of having a list of email subscribers is so that some of those subscribers will buy something from you one day.

That's probably quite clear to you already, but it's worth mentioning because there are people out there who think it's some sort of mortal sin to offer your email subscribers the opportunity to buy something.

And because at any given point in time, the vast majority of your email subscribers are *not* going to be ready to buy something from you, you need to offer them valuable content so they hang around until they *are* ready to buy something.

I call this B.B.B.: keeping your Brand in their Brain until they are ready to Buy.

Keep following my logic here.

We've got an email list of subscribers and we want them to buy something from you one day.

But we know that most of them are not ready to buy anything right now, so we need to keep your brand in their brain until they are ready to buy.

Clearly, given that they are "email" subscribers, the best medium through which to achieve our twin objectives of B.B.B. and having them buy something one day is to send them emails with good quality content and good quality offers.

The content-to-offer ratio (i.e. the number of times you offer valuable free content compared to the number of times you simply send them an offer to buy something) needs to be significantly stacked in favor of the free content as opposed to the buying offer.

A quick story to illustrate my point.

I met a guy once who was a retired Presbyterian church minister. Vic was his name.

He told me the story of his very first sermon at his very first church, where he had been charged with tending the souls of those who attended until they were ready to meet their Maker.

Vic said his very first sermon was full of fire and brimstone.

He promised them all eternal damnation, flickering flames licking at their nether regions, unspeakable anguish and pain and all the other things that I'm assuming hell comprises, unless they chose to stop being "Sunday Christians" and genuinely repent from their sins.

By the end of the service, he was feeling pretty pleased with himself.

He made his way from the pulpit out to the back room and walked briskly around the side of the church to the front door, ready to greet his parishioners as they exited from the church and into the bright daylight of the outdoors.

One after the other, the congregation members filed out of that church and shook his hand and smiled and offered some small talk and thanked him and congratulated him on a fine sermon.

The very last person exiting from the church was a bent, wizened old man, complete with walking stick and tartan cap on his head.

Vic was ready to gently clasp the man's skinny and wrinkled hand but instead the old man seized Vince's hand in a vice-like grip, crushing Vic's skin and knuckles under the strength of his handshake.

With a sharp intake of breath and tears of pain beginning to well up in his eyes, Vic composed himself, forced a feeble smile, and asked the old man if he had enjoyed the sermon.

The old man stared at Vic with his steely ice cold piercing blue-eyed eyes and with a broad Scottish accent said ...

"Sonny, if ye canna feed the sheep, dinna shear them."

And when it comes to your email list, never a truer word has been spoken.

The bottom line here is that you're going to have to send a significant volume of high-quality content opportunities to your email list.

We send out at least one podcast interview that I conduct each week.

And we send out at least two email invitations for my subscribers to attend an OPN Partner's webinar. The second one only goes out to those people who didn't register from the first email.

But still, that means the majority of some 25,000 email subscribers are receiving a minimum of three emails per week.

There are weeks that we'll send out up to seven emails with invitations for my subscribers to gain some value from a podcast or from a webinar or from some form of giveaway.

In a moment, you'll read about why this works so well even though currently you might be wondering why my email subscribers haven't simply unsubscribed.

There is a method to my madness, so keep reading. But until now, all you need to know is this: even with a great email subscriber list like I have, the marketing calendar still becomes the bottleneck.

And when your email subscribers are scattered all around the world, time zones add a further complication. That's because there is a good time and a bad time to send emails out, but it's way too complicated to send emails out by time zone segments.

What you need to do with your email list and your marketing calendar is to figure out which time zone you want to optimize the timing of your emails for.

I optimize for USA Eastern because North America is our primary beachhead.

And there's a simple reason why I optimize for North America and not for Europe.

In broad terms, and please forgive me for the sweeping generalization, but ...

Americans wake up in the morning wondering where they can spend their money.
Europeans wake up in the morning wondering where they can save their money.

And I know which type of market I'd prefer to optimize my marketing calendar for.

As mentioned elsewhere, I have Plan A and a Plan B for my OPN Partners, the former being a live webinar-swap and the latter being some form of static giveaway-swap.

The following marketing calendar reveals how I double my results by doubling the number of OPN Partners' reciprocal promotions that we can handle.

	Saturday	Sunday	Monday	Tuesday	Wednesday	Thursday	Friday
{Webinar} Partner 1	Email #1 4am/1am		Email #2 3pm/12pm	Webinar A 4pm/1pm			
{Webinar} Partner 2				Email#1 5pm/2pm		Email #2 4am/1am Webinar B 4pm/1pm	
{Give} Partner 1	Email #1 3pm/12pm		Email #2 4am/1am				
{Give} Partner 2			Email #1 10am/7am		Email #2 3pm/12pm		
{Give} Partner 3					Email #1 9pm/6apm		Email #2 3pm/12pm

You'll see that in any given week, this marketing calendar allows me to promote two OPN Partner webinars and three OPN Partner giveaways.

That's a lot of emails that I'm sending out, but you'll discover prior to the end of this chapter how I optimize email open rates and minimize unsubscribes through a very simple subject line technique.

In the meantime, I want to let you know that everything that I'm revealing in this book is proven over multiple years, but the marketing calendar as shown above is a more recent innovation and so I've only just started testing it. I wanted to disclose that so that you are aware it's possibly going to be a work in progress for the next few months. But I'm confident enough of its success to share it with you now.

And for our audio listeners, I'll include a copy of that marketing calendar along with the free downloads at **www. MarketingWithWebinars.com/Downloads/**

How to Build Your Email List Faster and With Subscribers Who Are More Likely to Buy

Start now (this minute)

The biggest single obstacle in the minds of my new clients is the idea that they can't engage in an OPN Partnership because they don't have an email list.

There are a bunch of reasons why this is simply an imagined impediment and not a real one.

For starters, we were all born naked.

None of us came out of our mom's womb with an email list attached.

The most important thing you can do for your business is to start an email list.

Go to any reputable CRM platform such as **www.mailchimp. com** or **www.mailer-lite.com** and sign up for a free account.

There is literally nothing to stop you from doing this right now.

It's free.

It's accessible.

So quit reading this book and go do it then come back and I'll take the next step.

Why are you still reading?

Seriously, go do that and then come back once you get yourself an online platform that you can populate with the email addresses of prospective clients.

Done it?

Hope so.

Now go and put a spreadsheet together and populate it with the first and last name and email address of every person that you've done business with or you have spoken to about doing business with since you were born.

The only caveat is that the dealings you had with those contacts have in some way been aligned to the type of product or service that you are currently marketing.

In other words, if you've had a dramatic shift in what you are marketing then the pre-shift contacts should *not* be loaded into your new email marketing platform/CRM.

Having got that out of the way, let me just say that I really don't care if you have five contacts in your new database or 50,000 contacts, provided they know you at least in some small measure and they know about your product or service.

Legally, in just about every province region and country in the world, having had contact with someone in a business context is sufficient for you to avoid running afoul of any spam laws when importing their details into your new CRM.

Of course, go and check your local spam legislation and any regulations in whatever associations you belong to and abide by the relevant laws and guidelines.

So now you have a list.

Like I said, I don't care how big it is. The important thing is to start. Now.

Almost all the people I conduct OPN Partner campaigns with care first and foremost about the quality of what you are going to offer their email subscribers, in the form of your webinar or giveaway, than they do about the size of your email list.

And we'll talk about how to put together a quality webinar presentation in the next chapter.

THE SPIRAL

This is an extension of my previous recommendation "start now."

Anyone can grow an email list fast.

They can just go out and buy an email list ethically and legally and avoiding any antispam laws.

There are a whole bunch of organizations that ask their new email subscribers if they'd like to hear from approved partners, and those organizations will often legitimately offer lists of their subscribers for sale.

The problem is that unless a person has opted into *your* email list for something *you* are offering that related to *your* product or service, then those contact details are virtually worthless.

Most people are horribly confused about what constitutes a lead.

Contact details such as names and email addresses are worthless on their own.

You can literally find a list of ten million contact details through our friends at Google Search. Platforms such as www.hunter.io specialize in identifying email addresses.

Contacts who have opted into another organization's email list that offers services or products that are close to yours *are* worth a little more — a lot more when that other organization recommends that those contacts check out your product or service.

And this is similar to what we are doing with an OPN Partnership.

You receive what is effectively a recommendation from a respected authority figure, or a respected brand, that by implication endorses your products and services.

OPN Partnerships are the fastest way I know of to grow a quality list.

And we can slice and dice these partnerships in various different ways. Here are just a few of them.

Webinar swap

The straight webinar swap, where you and your OPN partner promote each other's webinar to your email lists, is a terrific way to start growing your business relatively quickly and with high-quality subscribers.

You may start slower than people with bigger email lists but you'll Spiral up into larger lists as you complete each debrief as outlined above.

If you want more information on the concept of The Spiral, please refer to Pages 118 to 121 of my previous book "Inbound Marketing Book."

Webinar Panels

My favorite and all-time fastest way to grow a high-quality email list is the Webinar Panel method.

This involves you facilitating a webinar where you host three expert panelists who each get 15 minutes to share on their expertise.

What's in it for each panelist is exposure to the other panelists' Audiences.

Every panelist receives a list of all registrants and so each of them walks away from the webinar panel, at the very least, with more email subscribers for their email database.

And for the right people, that in and of itself is worth them investing their time on your Webinar Panel.

You'll also be allowing each panelist to provide contact details and probably a link for attendees to book a time and explore the idea of becoming a client of the panelist.

To get started, make a list of ten experts who target the same target market as you and who have a product or service that is similar to your own, but not the same.

For example, I am an inbound marketing specialist, so I might make a list of ten sales training experts.

Selling is not the same as marketing, but the two are closely aligned because marketers are experts at generating inquiries, whereas sales professionals are experts at converting those inquiries into clients.

Note that it's *not* critical to avoid people who market a product or service that's similar to your own. Mature professionals don't typically feel threatened by others who are experts in the same field.

By way of further example, a residential interior design specialist might put together a list of ten people including lighting experts, bathroom specialists, kitchen designers, and landscapers. The common denominator is that they are all targeting the same Audience, which is homeowners wanting to create a more livable home environment.

Hopefully, that gives you enough of an idea to start your list of ten experts. You can use Google search or search LinkedIn or go through the current network of contacts.

Finding experts is not difficult, especially if they're actively marketing because they will have a web presence.

Once you find an expert, make sure that you include their contact details as you compile your list of ten.

Most website owners are notoriously poor at responding to the "contact us" forms on their own website. Therefore, you're better off finding an email address or at the very least a LinkedIn profile link. Identifying their website should be easy enough, but if you can't find their email address, then use a service like **www.hunter.io** to find it. And around 60% of LinkedIn members make their email address public in the profile.

Once you have your ten experts listed, then run each through The Five Knockout Factors I listed above and ideally also through my algorithm at **www.JVjuice.com** to make as certain as possible that they'll be able to drive a significant number of registrants to your webinar panel.

Prioritize your list of potential panelists starting with those who you've identified as being the ones who can drive more registrants to your webinar panel than the others.

Approach them first. Explain the concept to them in a very short email.

Please read the last three words of the previous sentence again, this time very carefully.

That's right. Your initial approach must be a <u>very</u> short email.

Something like this will do:

> **Subject:** *Invitation to be a panelist on my webinar for [target market]*
>
> *Hi [firstname], I'm putting together a webinar panel of three experts in [name their service/product] and this short email is to see if you have an interest in being one of those three experts.*
>
> *Details have yet to be finalized but the benefit for you would be exposure to a potential Audience of hundreds of prospects along with a list of the webinar registrants which you could legitimately import into your existing CRM.*
>
> *At this stage all I need from you is an expression of interest or otherwise. Naturally I'm happy to receive any questions.*
>
> *Best, [sign off].*
>
> *[website, LinkedIn profile URL]*

Send an email to the first three people on your prioritized list and as soon as you have one that expresses an interest, then organize an online meeting with them to agree on a date that suits them for conducting the webinar panel.

That first person is going to attract others. The reason you agree to a date with the first panelist is to make sure that what you are planning does not conflict with their current commitments.

Plan your event around their schedule and not the other way around.

(The other option is to wait until you have your three panelists confirmed and then try and agree on a date that works for all of them. Don't do that; it's like trying to herd cats.)

Make sure you are explicit about the fact that each person involved in the webinar panel will receive a list of all registrants, including yourself. Full and open transparency is the best policy to ensure long-lasting relationships of trust with each of your panelists.

You can now email another three people on your list mentioning, with their prior approval, the name of the person who has already accepted your invitation to appear as a panelist.

Hopefully the first person who accepted your invitation is well known in the industry, because if they are, they will pull other people in like moths to a flame. Just keep inviting another three people every few days until you have three confirmed panelists.

Unfortunately, because books are not workshops, I can't give you every single detail of how you need to run this thing, but you can probably figure out most of the rest on your own.

However, you will need to draft a sequence of two email invitations that each panelist can send out to their respective email lists. In marketing speak, we call these the "swipe files."

Give each panelist permission to edit and refine and add their personal touch to the email invitations, but make sure that you have done the heavy lifting for them by writing the swipe file emails and setting up the registration page that will feature the panelist's photos and short bio plus a bullet-point checklist of the benefits of attending.

You'll also need to provide the webinar platform and you can see my recommendations for them in Chapter Seven.

There's a bit of work involved in setting up a Webinar Panel but relative to your other options, it's the best way to grow an email list very quickly, and one that's also good quality relative to your product or service niche.

At this stage, I'll bet dollars to donuts that you forgot about my debrief strategy that I mentioned previously.

Am I right?

Either way, make sure that you book a debrief with each of your webinar panelists so that you're able to ensure they were satisfied with their experience, and also flag in advance that you'll be interested in discussing referrals to other potential OPN Partners.

Remember: the debrief meeting is where most of the gold lies buried.

INFOSTACK (GIVEAWAY)

This is where a bunch of people get together and they each offer something that's perceived to be of value to each other's email list. Many contributors will offer a minicourse or an e-book or similar.

Almost exclusively, they are digital products that require an email subscription opt-in to access each individual piece of content.

The Infostack method can also be a great way to grow your email list relatively quickly and, in that regard, it will give you a similar outcome to the Webinar Panel strategy.

The difference, however, is that compared to the above strategy, the Infostack is more challenging to organize.

You may have seven or 12 or 20 or 30 contributors to organize before your launch deadline.

Personally, I wouldn't undertake such an exercise unless I delegated it to a willing team member who has more patience than me and who enjoys handling the organizational detail required.

Incidentally, notice that I used the phrase "perceived value."

Like everything in this world, an Infostack can be done very well and it can be done very badly.

Some Infostacks contain exceptionally poor-quality content and others contain genuinely valuable content, and of course that's two ends of a spectrum. But in order to make sure your brand builds credibility with each marketing campaign, you will want to be fussy about who you get involved if you decide to go down Infostack route.

Question: where is most of the gold buried in every Infostack?

Correct!

It's in the debrief.

Congratulations, now you're getting the hang of this.

Once you conclude your Infostack, make sure you set up a debrief with each contributor so you can ensure they were happy with the result and so you can cross-refer each other to proven OPN Partners.

How to Optimize Your Email Open Rates and Minimize Unsubscribes

It probably goes without saying that generating new client inquiries with webinars is a digital marketing strategy.

It therefore follows that generating registrants for each webinar is most efficient and effective when you also use a digital method.

As mentioned above, that inevitably means email invitations are going out to a lot of people on a regular basis.

My monthly objective for OPN Partner webinar swaps, prior to developing the marketing calendar referred to above, was four, and while that may be aspirational for your business as you read this, it's a pretty worthwhile objective to head toward.

Four OPN Partners to promote each month means one a week.

As you can imagine, that means I'm sending a lot of emails out to my email subscriber list every single week. In addition to sending out the first and second email invitation for my subscribers to attend the webinar of my OPN partner, I may also be sending out free giveaway opportunities from other OPN Partners (see "Plan B" below) as well as emails promoting various podcasts guests I've had on my podcast show.

That's a lot of emails going out every week to the same email subscribers.

Over the years, many people have expressed a concern about adopting a similar strategy because they're anxious about the number of unsubscribes they receive when they send so many emails.

If you feel some concern, my best advice to you is this:

Build your email list around your strategy, not your strategy around your email list.

My subscribers stay subscribed if they like receiving a lot of valuable free content in the form of podcasts, e-books and webinars.

I am increasingly fussy about the quality of the content from my OPN Partners that I expose my email subscriber list to. That means my email subscriber list knows that, if they receive an email from me recommending content from one of my partners, they can proceed with a reasonably high level of confidence that the content will be of good quality and that it contains valuable insights.

And at the time of this writing, I send back any affiliate checks that partners inadvertently send me so that I am not swayed by the potential dollars on offer when I'm considering the promotion of a prospective Partner's offer.

The real question that remains is not so much whether the content I am offering to my email subscribers from my OPN Partner is good quality (that should be a given), but rather whether it is *relevant* to my email subscribers needs at that very *minute* when they see the email from me with my OPN Partner's offer.

Therefore, I've developed a strategy so that every email subscriber can decide whether the content I'm offering in a promotional email is going to be relevant to their needs at that moment.

And they can make that decision in less than a second.

I came up with the strategy after I observed how I filtered the emails in my inbox.

Probably like you, I get 100 or more emails every day.

From my side, that's a deliberate strategy because I make a point of subscribing to a lot of email lists from people and organizations who target my target market. It's a great way for me to stay in touch with who is doing what and with whom. And I pick up a bunch of great OPN partners that way by popping their website address into **www.JVjuice.**

com and predetermining if they are a prospective partner who is in my "sweet spot."

But back to my strategy that allows my email subscribers to quickly determine whether something I'm offering them from an OPN partner will be of value to them at that particular time.

My observation of myself in filtering emails was that I would quickly glance at two factors which were firstly the sender and secondly the subject line.

Some senders I would instantly delete. They tended to be the emails from organizations as opposed to individuals. There were of course a few exceptions.

Once I had filtered by the sender, using the delete key on my keyboard, I then scanned the email subject line. I'm not one of these people who won't want to read every word of every email. I mean it's not like receiving an email is a novelty event anymore, like it used to be 25 years ago. We scan and delete and we always scan before we start reading. We don't just start reading. No one has the time for that anymore. There are too many emails and too many "better offers" in regard to how we use our time.

Once I noticed myself scanning for the sender's identity and then scanning the subject line before I decide whether to start reading an email, I decided to change my own formula for sending emails.

Mostly I send three types of emails to our list. The first one is when we release a new episode of our podcast. The second one is when we promote someone else's webinar, and the third one is when we promote someone else's giveaway.

Therefore, almost every email that we send out to our subscriber list starts with one of the following subject lines:

{7 MINUTE INTERVIEW}:

{WEBINAR}:

{GIVE}:

That allows my subscribers to instantly identify whether the email is about a podcast interview or a webinar or a free giveaway.

Next, we follow with a benefit-rich statement in the subject line. Here are some examples:

{7 MINUTE INTERVIEW}: Profit from Facebook Live

{WEBINAR}: Generate new clients from LinkedIn

{GIVE}: Ten point Instagram prospecting checklist

You'll see from the above formula that both the medium and the benefit can be identified in less than one second.

Since I adopted the above formula, our unsubscribes have dropped by just a smidgen over 50%.

They were never high in the first place.

For example, when our list was at around 6,000 subscribers, which is when I developed the above formula, we were averaging 15 unsubscribes per email blast.

But even though our unsubscribe numbers weren't high to start with, I'll still take a reduction of over 50% any day of the week, thank you very much.

My number two tip for using emails as a promotional medium

Once you've made it easy and fast for an email subscriber to identify what it is you're offering them, the next best thing you can do is make sure that your call to action is "above the fold."

This means that they don't have to scroll or page down in order to know what it is you're asking them to do.

I have a friend who's a brilliant copywriter and will often write three screens / pages of the story before he gets to his point. His emails talked about when he was a kid sitting by the river at his father's knee fishing, described the stream as a babbling brook and the sun kissing his forehead while his father's deep gravelly voice converted some sage piece of advice and so on, and so on, and so on. I don't know about you, but me, if I'd wanted a novel, I would've gone to the Amazon store.

So, whatever it is you want your reader to do, let them know right near the top of your email what that thing is.

Whether that's clicking a link to register for a webinar, or to click and download an e-guide, or to click replay with your question or whatever. Make sure they don't have to scroll down or read through screen after screen in order to try and figure out what the heck it is you want them to do.

Some people, like the friend I mentioned above, confuse the context, and context should always determine your method.

Maybe they have gone to a copywriting workshop (a great idea, by the way) and learned about sales pages. They are taught, quite rightly, that if a prospect has an interest in a certain subject, they will want to read in-depth about that subject.

That's why a lot of the sales pages on websites will go on for screen after screen after screen.

But the context is a sales page on the website where readers are thinking about spending their hard-earned money, and that means they want all the information they can get in order to feel confident that their investment will be worthwhile.

The method of "long copy" as it's called is therefore appropriate when someone wants to dive deep into your offer.

But an email is not a sales page. The context is completely different. With an email people want and need to get to your bottom line fast.

So keep your email short and your sales pages long.

As a side note, I have long sales pages (e.g. www.iWantSolo. com) but I always try and remember to still keep the call to action as close to the top of the screen as possible.

In my experience, some people just want the bottom line and they want it really fast and don't want to have to go hunting for it. I call these people The Seekers, and by my estimation, they make up about 3% of my website visitors.

Then there's The Explorers who make up around 12%, and they want to read every word of a 12- or 15-page sales letter.

Therefore, I build my sales pages to cater to both Audiences by having all the key information summarized near the top of the webpage, but providing a lot of detail "below the fold" for those who want to delve deeper.

If you want more information on the three different types of Audiences, being The Seekers and The Explorers and The Wanderers and how to boost your results by approximately five times by catering to each of these three Audience categories, then please refer to my book *Leadsology®: Marketing The Invisible* and The SEW Segmentation Formula that I cover in pages 245 to 254.

How to Develop a Plan B so You Maximize Marketing Opportunities

A webinar swap with a qualified OPN Partner is what I call "Plan A."

It's my preferred modus operandi. It's the number one thing that I'm going for with my carefully selected potential OPN Partner.

But a webinar swap is not always going to fit every prospective OPN partner's timing.

So it pays to have a Plan B Asset to cross-market to each other's email lists, and the easiest Plan B Asset is the one-page giveaway.

85% of your website visitors will simply want to dip their toe in the water of your brand.

With as little skin in the game as possible.

And that does means they don't want to book a time to talk with you about becoming a client, and it means they aren't ready to buy whatever product or service you have, straight off the bat.

It's the equivalent of speed dating where they want just a few minutes at your table, before they decide if they want a real date with you.

"Softly, softly catchee monkey" as the saying goes.

It therefore pays dividends to have what I call the "Short Simple and Shiny" (SSS) giveaway that you can offer those website visitors as well as the subscribers of your OPN Partners who don't want to conduct a webinar swap for whatever reason.

Your SSS giveaway could be a mind map, a checklist, a template, a blueprint, or model, just to name a few possibilities.

Always make it one page and always make sure, when you offer it, that people understand it requires very little time for them to consume.

You can see an example of this at **www.leadsology.guru/ the-model/** where I offer a one-page interactive model for the 85% of my website visitors who simply want something that short, simple, and shiny.

Another great example of this is to be found at the very clever Laura Posey's website **https://simplesuccessplans.com/ daily/** where you can download her daily success template.

Hopefully, between my example and Laura's, you'll gain some inspiration for how to create your own Short Simple and Shiny giveaway.

Then you'll have a Plan B, whereby you can promote an OPN Partner's Short Simple and Shiny thing and they can promote yours.

Plan A is a one-step method and Plan B is a two-step method.

With Plan A, your OPN partner invites their subscribers to attend your webinar.

I'll explain in the next chapter why the webinar is your best option for generating very high-quality new client inquiries. In the meantime, please just trust me when I say that getting new email subscribers to attend your webinar is your most profitable strategy.

As mentioned, Plan B is a two-step method.

You first get subscribers from your OPN partner's email list to subscribe to your email list in exchange for downloading your Short Simple and Shiny thing.

As soon as they have downloaded your SSS, they will receive an automated email welcoming them to your community.

You explain to them in that welcome email that you'll send them invitations to attend webinars and other special events and special offers.

And you should invite them to unsubscribe and make it easy for them to do so, if receiving offers is not something they want. (By the way, the more explicit you make your invitation for them to unsubscribe the less unsubscribes you'll have.)

Then, five days before your next webinar, you'll invite them to register and attend.

That's why I call Plan B a two-step method.

Step one is them opting in for your Short and Simple Shiny thing, and step two is you inviting them to attend your webinar.

You should lead all of your prospects to your webinar before you offer them the opportunity to meet and discuss working together. That way, all your new client inquiry meetings will be with people who are motivated, qualified, and educated about how you work with your clients.

Chapter Three:

How To Create And Deliver A Powerfully Persuasive Presentation

I<small>T'S</small> <small>IMPOSSIBLE FOR</small> anyone to truly appreciate the science and skill involved in any specialist pursuit, until they have a crack at it themselves.

You can watch your favorite golfer or your favorite tennis player or your favorite opera singer or whoever for as long as you like, but until you pick up that club or that racket or try belting out your own Aria, you'll never truly appreciate how much time and effort and skill is involved in delivering a consummate performance.

The map is not the territory, as they say. The theory is not the reality and the observation is most definitely not the performance.

All of which is to say that you would be wise not to underestimate what goes into creating and delivering a truly powerful presentation.

If you attend one of my webinars, you'll see what I hope you'll agree is a reasonable standard of presentation.

But even if you're impressed, you won't truly understand why I did what I did and when I did it let alone how I did it.

Therefore, in this chapter I want to pull back the curtain that would normally exist between you as a webinar attendee and me as a webinar presenter so you have a better shot at creating and delivering your own powerfully persuasive presentation.

Having said that, and in the interests of full disclosure, this chapter is not a *workshop,* nor is it a step-by-step *program* that can guide you through the process of creating and delivering a powerfully persuasive presentation.

It simply can't be, because it's a book, not any of those other mediums which are designed for detailed instructions and guided implementation. For that (detailed instructions and guided implementation), the unvarnished truth is that you'll need to work with me or someone else you trust.

But this section will certainly give you key insights that will not only prove to be valuable in their own right, but will also elevate your awareness that, if you want to create something that truly is effective, you need to put in a bit of work.

Creating a powerfully persuasive presentation gives you leverage.

Once you have developed your Core Marketing Asset, being the presentation, you can use that Asset like any other asset: to profit from the same investment, time and again for decades to come, in this case in the form of generating bulk leads in less than one hour, that being the duration of your presentation.

Because every time you present your webinar, you'll be doing so to an Audience of multiple attendees. You may start with six or eight attendees, but if you follow my system faithfully, you'll end up with 600 or 800 attendees at some of your webinars.

And that's when you'll be able to begin generating six figures and even potentially seven figures of revenue every month.

All without leaving home.

THE NUMBER ONE OBJECTIVE OF EVERY WEBINAR

In my previous book, *Inbound Marketing Book*, I outline The Eight Objectives which every webinar presenter should seek to achieve.

But seven of those objectives are secondary compared to the number one objective, which is to explicitly establish your capability of delivering on the promise in the title of your webinar.

The title of your webinar must be expressed in a manner which explicitly offers a benefit to the attendee.

A recent title I saw was:

"Five Future Trends For Marketing Webinars"

That may invoke some interest or curiosity, but there is zero explicit benefit expressed in that title and it's only likely to attract die-hard webinar presenters like me, and if I had a better offer for the use of my time, then I would feel zero compulsion to attend.

But compare that title with something like this one:

"How My Clients In 27 Cities And 15 Time Zones Around The World

Are Using Webinars To Generate Inbound New Client Inquiries Virtually Every Week Of The Year."

You'll probably agree that the second title is more compelling than the first.

While the former invokes a little curiosity, the latter does the same in much greater measure while also promising an explicit benefit in the form of high-quality new client inquiries on a weekly basis.

So assuming that you craft a benefit-rich title that will get cut-through in the minds of your ideal clients, then the most important thing that you can do after that is to establish beyond a shadow of a doubt, during your webinar, that you have the capability to deliver on the promise in that title.

Not surprisingly, the second title that I've offered above, is from my own webinar.

Therefore, my most important objective is to demonstrate that I have the capability to work with my clients and generate a weekly flow of high-quality new client inquiries.

In the Persuasion Sequence Template that I reveal below, I'll show you how I do that.

COMMON BUT COSTLY MISTAKES TO AVOID

But first I want to save you a lot of time and a lot of effort and I want to help you avoid the frustration and disappointment that will inevitably follow your webinar if you mess it up with anyone of the following mistakes.

Please read this section carefully because you only gain great clarity around how to do a thing (in this case how to create and present a powerfully persuasive presentation) if you also understand how not to do a thing.

Like you I'm sure, I appreciate the value that lies in learning from other people's mistakes rather than learning from our own.

Thinking it's a training webinar

Marketing and training are two different things.

Marketing is what I do before I have a client and training is what I do after I have a client.

Don't be misled by the plethora of people who offer a "training webinar" when they are actually presenting a marketing webinar. They are the digital equivalent of the wolf in sheep's clothing. Bait and switch. You think you are getting training, but you are getting a low-value pitch.

So don't follow them or make them believe that your webinar is about providing information and/or the application of that information.

A marketing webinar is far more about motivation, identification, and qualification than it is about information.

You want to motivate the right people to reach out and contact you or to wisely invest in your products or services. That's the motivation part.

The identification part is that you want those "right people" to know who they are so that you don't get the wrong ones making inquiries. And by "the wrong ones" I mean those who (a) *can't afford* to work with you, or those for whom (b) your service or product is *not a fit*, or for whom (c) the *timing is not right*.

And that leads us nicely to the qualification part, which is where, having motivated and identified the right people, you clearly communicate to them the characteristics they must possess in order for you and them to enter into a mutually beneficial business transaction.

Being boring

If it's not captivating, it's not marketing.

Someone once said that the worst sin in marketing is being boring. I believe that's close to the truth but it's probably only the second-worst sin in marketing.

I have seen webinar presentations that have resulted in a flood of sales from presenters who I considered to be deadly boring but who did managed to convince their Audience that they had the capability to deliver on the promise that was inherent in their webinar title.

Therefore, being boring is the second-worst thing you can do, with a failure to convince your Audience that you have relevant capability being the worst sin.

After convincing your Audience of your capability, Captivation is your second most-important objective.

If you speak in a monotone and practice the infamous "death by PowerPoint" by having Audience members sit through bullet point of text after bullet point of text, then it's far less likely you'll have a rush of inquiries or sales at the end of your presentation.

The latest buzzword in the world webinars is "interaction."

This is the idea that the Audience can interact with you as the presenter. And it's a great concept. You can use questions and polls and surveys during a presentation to generate a response from your Audience.

But bear in mind please that the concept of interaction is a subset of Captivation.

Captivation is defined as being in a state of intense interest or fascination.

A bit like a spell or a trance or enchantment.

It's a psychological state induced by a presentation (in this case) that captures the attention of your Audience. It's the gold standard of webinar presentations and it's one that you should and must aspire to.

So, use polls, questions, and surveys to create Audience interaction, but don't leave it there. Strive for constant Captivation and not just periodic interaction.

Other ways to generate Captivation include the use of stories, metaphors, analogies, similes, and examples and I'll cover that in a moment with The Concept Conveyor.

One of the webinars that I present is specifically for professionals offering a service or advice. That includes management consultants and executive or business coaches. A key point that I drive home during that particular presentation is that no one is going to buy from them until they establish The Four Levels Of Psychological Allure which, as a reminder, are Respect and Rapport and Relatability and Reciprocity.

I could just tell my Audience that they need to establish those four levels but it's not especially Captivating.

Instead, I tell my Hugh Jackman story. It's about the time I asked my wife who she thought was the world's most irresistible man.

I explain to my Audience that she thought about it for a moment and then came up with Hugh Jackman.

I then tell my Audience that I had a follow-up question for my wife which was "if Hugh Jackman came to the front door right now and knocked on it, and you opened it and he proposed marriage to you, what would you say?."

I relate how my wife blushed and apologized but, truthful woman that she is, told me that she probably would run away with him.

I then explain how I told her she didn't have to apologize because the guy is such a hunk and such an amazing all-round human being, that if *I'd* opened the front door and he proposed to *me*, I'd probably run away with him too, and I'm not even gay. I mean, it's Hugh Freaking Jackman!

Of course, the Audience has a bit of a laugh about the story and then I bring them to the point of the story, which is that most of us are not the commercial equivalent of Hugh Jackman, and that we better offer our prospects a "first date" before we "propose" working together.

That's a relevant example of how you can use the story to illustrate a point instead of directly telling an Audience what the point is.

Another example: One of my clients is targeting the owners of businesses with $5 million or more in revenue.

Tim (my client) says that the owner of such a business may be suffering from a lack of management and leadership skills and would prefer to have their business running as smooth as silk, continually generating more revenue while he is being able to enjoy more free time.

So, in Tim's presentation, when he wants to establish Relatability, he talks about "Whack-A-Mole Management."

Whack-A-Mole, if you don't already know, is an arcade game where you use a mallet to try and whack a mole which jumps out of one of a dozen holes in the top of the arcade game.

No sooner do you see a mole jumping out of the hole and try and whack it, then the mole disappears, and another mole jumps out of another hole. Unless you are fast, you spend the entire three minutes whacking fresh air.

And a lot of managers feel like they going to work every day to play Whack-A-Mole, where no sooner do they fix the problem of a team member not showing up (whack) then a customer complaint comes in (whack) or suppliers let them down (whack).

Tim could describe those sorts of scenarios directly, but it wouldn't have nearly the same impact that it does by using the Whack-A-Mole simile.

Another example. When I explain how inbound marketing works versus outbound marketing, I don't give people a dry and technical definition.

I ask them to imagine a forest in which there are 100 sleeping Grizzly bears.

I explain to them that we somehow magically know that three of the sleeping bears are hungry.

And I asked my Audience to imagine that they had a pot of honey and that their objective was to find the three hungry bears and have them enjoy the pot of honey.

I point out that the sleeping bears are a metaphor for prospects and that their honeypot is a metaphor for their product or service.

As I'm explaining this imaginary scenario, my slide deck is changing to show images of the forest and the sleeping bears and the pot of honey.

Having explained to my Audience that their objective is to find the three hungry bears from among the hundred sleeping bears, and to have those three bears enjoy their honey, I give them two options.

Option one is to grab a big long pole and sharpen one end and then go running through the forest, find a sleeping bear and jab the bear in the backside with the sharp end of the pole.

That will wake the bear up and if they are lucky and the bear is one of the three hungry ones, then the bear's hunger will exceed its anger and it will therefore eat the honey and not the person who stuck a sharp pole up their rear.

But I also point out that, if they are not so lucky and it's one of the 97 sleeping bears who are not hungry, then they had better be a really fast runner.

That way I draw a parallel between cold calling and outbound marketing, which is like running through a forest and annoying bears that have no interest in the honey. That's like cold calling or pestering people who have no interest in a particular product or service.

I then explain to them that option two is to simply put their honeypot outside the forest. The three sleeping bears that were hungry would probably start dreaming they were swimming in honey but then they'd wake up, probably a little bit disappointed. But then they'd smell the honey and that would make them come out of the forest and eat it.

I draw a parallel between that second scenario and inbound marketing and demonstrate how it's possible to generate inquiries from people who are "hungry" for a certain product or service by offering a sample.

Once again, instead of communicating an idea to my Audience in plain English, I've used an analogy, containing some metaphors (bears = prospects, honey = product sample) and I've got my message across in a manner which is far more Captivating than simply telling them my point directly.

I'll reveal more ways to Captivate your Audiences in Chapter Six, but for now I recommend you think less about including long lists of bullet-point text in your presentations and more about using images and metaphors and similes and stories and examples.

All the great teachers have used these devices to make their point.

Mohammed did it, Christ did it, Buddha did it.

Each of these people, in turn, influenced generations across thousands of years and they did it by using stories and metaphors and similes and parables in their presentations.

And interestingly, despite collectively generating billions of followers, neither one wrote even one word. All they offered to their Audiences were powerfully persuasive presentations.

Success leaves clues.

The enemy of motivation is complication

Having trained hundreds of clients on how to put together a powerfully persuasive presentation, I can tell you categorically that the biggest trap that most people fall into is making their presentation complicated.

"If you want to make a lot of money,

And build a great big reputation,

Take something that's actually quite simple,

And add a big complication,"

I wrote that little ditty many years ago to highlight a trend amongst experts who felt insecure about delivering presentations. Adding unnecessary complication only serves to have people scratching their head and telling themselves that they will have to go away and think about it some more.

The only time you want people to go away and think about a thing is when you tell him that you want them to go away and think about a thing.

Other than that, you don't want them scratching their head.

Rather, you want to be able to explain how you work with your clients and how they could potentially work with you in a manner which is clear and simple and easy to understand.

As the old benchmark goes, "if a 12-year-old can't understand, then it's too complicated."

The desire to add complexity to a presentation is often triggered by worrying about making your presentation bulletproof to a critique from your contemporaries.

And if you were presenting to your contemporaries, that's probably a reasonable concern.

But as always, context is everything.

The context of you creating a powerfully persuasive presentation is an Audience full of your prospective ideal clients, *not* an Audience full of your contemporaries.

The scientist wanting to have their research published in a peer-reviewed journal better have the paper very well thought through.

But that same scientist explaining to me why I should invest in their next cancer research project had better make it very simple and easy for me to understand.

Your Audience is your context and your context determines your content.

Let me give you another example to bring this to life.

There are exactly 51 steps that a client of mine needs to take in order to embed an inbound lead generation system, using webinars and OPN, into their business.

Yes, 51 is a lot but we have them take small steps and we sequence them so that it's easier and faster and simpler for them to implement.

Nevertheless, the fact remains that 51 is a daunting number for those who don't yet understand that we make the whole process simpler and easier and faster to implement due to the fact that I spent over $100,000 with professional Instructional Designers to make my program simpler and easier and faster to implement.

That's all very well and good for a new client who signs up and starts my program, because they can see that it is relatively simpler and easier and faster to implement.

But if I told my webinar Audiences, some of whom I'm hoping will become clients, that there were 51 steps that they needed to implement, then I doubt very much that I would generate many inquiries, let alone many new clients.

Therefore, when I get to the part of my webinar where I'm explaining to my clients how my inbound lead generation model works, I take the 51 steps and summarize them into three.

Those three parts include that they are going to need to find an **Audience** and that they will want an **Asset** through which to get the message about their product or service out to that Audience. And I explain that they will also need a call to **Action**.

If one of my marketing colleagues were to review my webinar, they could quite rightly suggest that I hadn't revealed all the detail of my model.

But remember, I'm not looking to build a powerfully persuasive presentation for my contemporaries or colleagues, but rather for Audiences that are relatively uneducated and whom I would lose if I explained exactly what they need to do in detail.

There's an old consulting saying, "never confuse promise with delivery."

Another twist on that would be to say "never confuse marketing with client work."

They are two different things.

What you need to communicate to a prospect in order to have them move to become a client, is very different from what you would then have to communicate to that client in order for them to receive full value.

Remember: context first, content second.

Your Audience is the context, not some imaginary colleague who sits on your shoulder. So, create your content to match that context.

Revealing text and talking using different words simultaneously

Most of my webinars will include a few bullet points with text.

As you probably gathered from the above, I do minimize the amount of text that I use in my presentations because a lot of text is more useful in a training context, not in a marketing context.

Nevertheless, it's likely that you're going to be including some text.

But make sure that you never reveal a large body of text if you want your Audience to assimilate what you want to communicate.

The only exception to this rule is where you deliberately want to impress on your Audience how comprehensive a thing is, but that exception is rare indeed.

So, assuming you understand the importance of not revealing a large body of text, that still leaves us with the odd set of bullet points with text that you might want to reveal.

And that brings me to my point: for the majority of your Audience, a visual input will override an auditory input.

What that means in plain English is that if you reveal a bullet point and text, the minds of your Audience will be occupied with reading that text and they will not hear what you say other than if you are also verbalizing the text in sync with them reading it.

For example here's a bullet point from one of my past webinars:

■ Other valid Audience options include SEO

If I click my little mouse button and that text comes sliding onto the screen, then I will read it out loud at exactly the same time that I reveal it to my Audience. And I will read it word for word, exactly as it is appearing on the screens of my Audience.

MARKETING WITH WEBINARS

By contrast, if I were to reveal that text and instead of read-ing it word by word, I began explaining what I mean or if I were to give an example, then at best, virtually none of my Audience would be hearing my words.

And at worst, I'd simply confuse my Audience by asking them to comprehend both a visual input as well as an au-ditory input that were conflicting with each other for their attention.

This is an incredibly common presentation mistake that de-rails your message and confuses Audiences.

So, if you do have a slide that contains text then reveal only one bullet point at a time and read the text out loud, word by word at exactly the same time that your Audience is see-ing the text.

Once you have read the text, then you can go on to elaborate or give examples or tell your story and so on.

Amateurish formatting and graphics

In the previous section, I mentioned that if a 12-year-old can't understand your presentation then you need to redo it.

But that's not to say that your presentation should look like it was a 12-year-old who put it together!

I'm not going to write a lot about this, but suffice it to say that, unless you personally can put together a presentation that looks world-class, then you best go to www.upwork.com and find a freelancer to make your presentation visually world-class.

100 | TOM POLAND

And although I am a big fan of hiring freelancers from countries like India and Bangladesh, it's very difficult to find a freelancer there who understands the visual culture of say North America, the United Kingdom, or Australia unless they have been raised in a Western culture. A presentation that looks fresh out of a Bollywood movie would probably do very well in New Delhi, but it won't do so well in New York. Conversely, if I were presenting to an Indian Audience, I wouldn't hire a New Yorker to put the presentation together.

Remember: context first (in this case, your Audience's culture), content second.

Overcomplicating your funnel

I believe there are literally millions of aspiring marketers the world over who never get started simply because they are daunted by the level of complexity that some trainers suggest they need to cope with in order to enjoy the profits that flow from a well-constructed online funnel.

Some teachers recommend that you run Facebook advertisements and that you split test those advertisements with different colors and titles and figure out which advertisement pulls better than the other.

You then kill off the loser and replace it with a challenger to your champion.

Rinse and repeat.

Ad infinitum.

Ad nauseum.

Pretty much for the rest of eternity.

They'll also recommend that you split-test the two landing pages that those two advertisements lead people to.

Again they'll say that you want to split test the colors and the titles and the images and the wording.

Kill off the loser and replace it with a challenger to your champion.

Rinse and repeat.

For all eternity.

Then they'll talk about tripwires and segmentation and auto responders and offers and price points and drop-down offers and upsell offers and the list of final components goes on and on and on.

Kill off the loser and replace it with a challenger to your champion.

Rinse and repeat.

For all eternity.

Maybe it works. Maybe it doesn't.

I've set them up and some of them worked well and some of them didn't.

We could debate all of that, but let me just tell you this as a certainty: setting up a complicated online funnel is a job for someone who has a much greater capacity to handle complication than my poor little simple brain possesses.

And you don't really need complicated online funnels.

Online funnel marketers often lure their new clients in with the promise that the funnel can be "set it and forget it." That you'll be able to create your funnel and then just sit on the beach all day and simply poke a couple of keys on your laptop for maybe half an hour a day and see all the money flooding into your bank account.

The perversely funny thing about online funnels is that, if you set one up, you'll spend less time at the beach than ever before because you'll be burning the midnight oil every night killing off the losers and building another challenger. All the while stressing about whether Mark Zuckerberg is going to increase you Cost Per Click (CPC) another buck per click.

Rinse and repeat, every day.

For the rest of eternity.

To those who decide to build a Facebook / Linkedin / You-Tube / Instagram / TikTok advertising funnel: good luck with that plan.

You have probably heard of the Pareto principle.

That's where an Italian statistician by the name of, you guessed it, Pareto, was hired by the British government to survey the distribution of wealth in England.

He discovered that 80% of the wealth was owned by 20% of the citizens.

He further discovered that 95% of the wealth was in the hands of 5% of the citizens.

He went on to survey many other countries and found the same ratios applied right across Europe.

The Pareto Principle, or the 80-20 Principle as it has become known, has held true across a surprising number of non-wealth-related areas including manufacturing, sales, quality control, logistics and supply and many other disciplines. Read Richard Koch's marvelous book "The 80/20 Principle" if you want to indulge in the mind-blowing potential afforded to each and every one of us by applying the Pareto Principle to our work and our love life.

And 80/20 applies to your marketing efforts as well. You'll get 80% of the results with 20% of the effort by following my recommended model.

It's equally true that if you want to get the other 20% of the results that you won't get with my model, you'll need to expand 80% more time and 80% more effort and 80% more money in the pursuit of that remaining 20%.

That's your call, but if you're into the most efficient use of your resources, then I urge you to apply the 80-20 Principle to your marketing efforts and just stick to marketing with webinars and the OPN model that I've outlined in the previous chapter.

My funnel is very simple: **OPN** to **Webinar** to **Inquiry**.

That simple funnel captures 80% of the leads with only 20% of the effort and cost that capturing 100% would require.

My final word on complicated online funnels is this: never hire a PhD or an MBA graduate to build your funnel. You will end up with a monster of complexity that consumes itself until the whole thing self-destructs.

This is with rare exception.

THE PERSUASION SEQUENCE: MY SLIDE BY SLIDE EXAMPLE OF A MARKETING WEBINAR PRESENTATION

In this section, I'll walk you through a Persuasion Sequence using slides from my own marketing webinar.

I've included screenshots to illustrate each agenda item and if you are listening to the audio version of this book, you won't miss out because I've included the complete, uncut edition of my presentation in the free downloads of the presentation slides at **www.MarketingWithWebinars.com/Downloads/**.

For the sake of simplicity in this book however, I've cut some slides out in the following section.

Your title slide

This is where you present your core value proposition.

The title must contain the explicit benefit for attending your online presentation and it must present that benefit in a manner that is differentiated so that it gets the attention of your ideal client.

A case in point is the title of my current presentation which is as follows:

DEMONSTRATION

How Our Clients Across 19 Time Zones

Are Generating Weekly New Client Inquires

* Predictably   * Inbound   * Quality   * Simple   * Inexpensive

A lot of people make the mistake of thinking that the title of your online presentation needs to be the same as your unique sales proposition (USP) or elevator pitch.

But the reality is that, with the title for a presentation, you get a lot more "real estate" to play with than you do with either a USP or an elevator pitch.

And if you can use those extra words to increase the appeal of your benefit, then use it you should.

I could have a title slide that simply said: "A New Lead Generation Method" and that would be accurate, but I would not get the cut-through that I achieved by articulating the benefit of attending in clearer and more specific terms.

One of my best tips for creating a title that gets cut-through and increases desire is to include specificity.

When you do it right, specificity increases desirability and believability.

For example, you'll notice that in my title I've included the fact that I have clients in 27 cities and 15 time zones around the world. Also note the words "inbound" and "weekly."

That sort of specificity greatly enhances the perception of differentiation, and that in turn gets me more cut-through (more attention) than by simply writing about lead generation in a more general way.

Also note that I've included the duration of the presentation and the fact that there will be a question-and-answer session. These are not essential elements, but they help increase certainty for the registrant in terms of their commitment (the duration) and enhances their perceived benefit (the Q&A).

In summary, make sure that your title sounds different from whatever your competitors are offering and that it's benefit-rich and that it contains specifics.

And as alluded to previously, position your presentation as a demonstration and not a free training webinar, so you show transparency and directness to your potential clients, right from the get-go.

Then comes the main agenda slide.

AGENDA

1. Who will benefit
2. Why listen to me?
3. What's the promise?
4. Where's the proof?
5. Inbound Lead Generation
6. Best practice: Inbound Marketing
7. Want to implement?
8. Q&A

And every time I click through to a new agenda item during my presentation, the upcoming section is highlighted in red, as follows:

AGENDA

1. Who will benefit
2. Why listen to me?
3. What's the promise?
4. Where's the proof?
5. Inbound Lead Generation
6. Best practice: Inbound Mark‹
7. Want to implement?
8. Q&A

This provides the Audience with a series of "milestones" that tell them how far we've come, and how far we have to go. People need certainty and they want to feel a sense of progress and milestones are a great way to meet each of those needs.

Agenda item 1: Who will benefit

Every agenda item introduces the purpose of each part of your presentation.

And often, each agenda item is an opportunity for you to repeat the promise that's embedded in the title of your presentation.

Having said that, the specific reason for agenda item number one is to give people confidence that they are in the right place and to assure them that they are going to obtain the value they came for.

I only use one slide to achieve this and it looks like this:

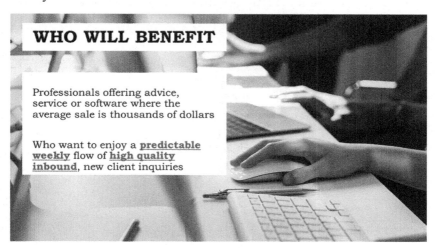

That slide also gives me the opportunity to repeat the benefit of working with me and ramps up my attendees' motivation levels just a bit more.

Agenda item 2: Why Listen To Me?

Because the terms "marketing" and "bullsh*t" are practically synonymous in the minds of many in my Audience, it's incumbent upon me to state in clear and specific terms why I'm different from the merchants of hype that they have had the misfortune to experience in the past.

And I mean, isn't it a great question? Why *should* people listen to me?

Frankly, unless I can answer that question in a manner which is both clear and convincing, then I don't deserve to occupy an hour of my Audience's time.

"Why Listen To Me?" consists of five slides in my presentation.

The first slide has an images of some of the books that I've written.

Most of my clients haven't written books, so they replace those images with their logo or anything else that's graphically relevant and impressive.

When I click and reveal that slide, I talk for no more than 15 seconds.

The next slide mentions some global luminaries who I have shared the stage with, and I briefly identify each one as I reveal their photos, ending up with mine. From left to right, they are Dr Ivan Misner, Richard Koch and Michael Gerber.

Again, this is like cream on the cake, so if you can't drop brand names like this, just skip it.

As I talk about my background, I only mention experience that is relevant to lead generation.

I don't include any other successful experience or any other type of positive results that I have helped clients achieve in almost four decades, other than what is relevant to the subject of lead generation.

And in almost 40 years of sales and marketing, I also developed expertise in disciplines such as human resources, strategic planning, project management and a host of other leadership and management skills. But none of them are mentioned other than those that are related to my marketing capability.

So don't bore your attendees with where you graduated from unless you need to reinforce the fact that you have academic qualifications that support the idea that you know what you're talking about when it comes to delivering the promise that's embedded in your title slide.

After the slides of my book and the speakers that I've shared stages with, I explain that none of that is reason enough to listen to me and what is far more important than my bio are my clients' results, and I very quickly reveal three slides that represent three main target markets for me.

RESULT: C-SUITE EXECS

Thanks to the Leadsology® model, **I now have a full pipeline of new client inquiries** from Directors and C-Suite Execs of some of the world's biggest food corporations including Coca-Cola, Mars and Unilever.

Derek Roberts
Consultant

RESULT: SME/SOLO

Thanks to Tom Poland, I'm now **generating five times the number of new clients** than previously and in less time than I ever thought possible.

Christina Force
Coach / Trainer

RESULT: RETIREMENT MARKET

I thought I'd hit a ceiling but thanks to Tom Poland's program **I've gone from $600,000 to over $1,000,000 in annual fees**. I'm delighted!

Greg Moyle
Financial Planner

If you have explicit and benefit-rich testimonials from clients, then use them, but make them short and to the point. Otherwise you can swap those slides out with the story of your own journey that led you where you are today.

I started with zero books, zero speaking gigs, and zero testimonials and I still enjoyed great results. These devices are just cream on the cake of captivating content. They help but they are not the main act.

Still, there are other ways to achieve the objective of establishing your capability of being able to deliver on the promise inherent in your title.

Telling your story is one of the latest and greatest trends in marketing.

I haven't jumped on board that bandwagon very often, however storytelling is a terrific way to establish relatability with an Audience and to reinforce your capability.

With storytelling, you can talk about where you *were* at (where your Audience is probably at as they listen to you) and where you are *now* at (where your Audience wants to get to, hopefully with your help when they become a client).

"I was fat and/or unhealthy and now I am slim and/or healthy."

"I was broke and now I am wealthy."

"My teams were underperforming and now they are over-performing."

Storytelling is particularly relevant if you're launching a new business and you don't have a bunch of powerfully explicit benefit-rich testimonials that you can reveal on the other three slides that are a part of the agenda item "Why Listen To Me?"

But because I have a lot of successful clients who have volunteered benefit-rich testimonials, I use those instead of telling my story about how I searched the world for effective inbound lead generation methods but came up short, and how I used to be broke but, once I figured out inbound lead generation, I became wealthier and more successful.

Agenda item 3: What's The Promise?

Neuro Linguistic Programming (NLP) and those that went before it, including Maxwell Maltz (*Psycho Cybernetics*), Dennis Waitley (*The Psychology of Winning*), all tell us that it's very difficult for the unconscious mind to distinguish between a thing that is vividly imagined and a thing that is real.

The opportunity with this agenda item is to paint a picture in the minds of the attendee that has them imagine the transformation they'll experience after they are finished working with you.

To be clear, this is not a matter of having them imagine being what it's like to work with you, but rather the benefit that follows from having done so.

In order to stimulate their imagination, you need to not only describe the benefit of having worked with you; you will also need to describe the sensory experience of that transformation by telling them what they will feel or see or hear or smell or taste, depending which senses are the most relevant.

Here is what's on the slide that I use to bring to life the promise that I make, once a client has implemented my method:

THE PROMISE

You wake up Monday morning and while sipping your coffee, you open your calendar and you feel a smile spread across your face as you see bookings from prospective Ideal Clients who want to know more about working with you and...

1. These bookings are <u>inbound</u>

2. They <u>know your fee range</u>

3. The <u>timing is good</u> for them

4. They hope <u>to confirm</u> you have what they need

Notice how I create a picture and the experience in their mind of sipping their coffee.

I also invoke the physical sensation of feeling a smile spread across their face.

And I make use of their visual sense as well by having them imagine looking at their calendar.

And then I stack the benefits in a way that the most successful infomercials do, by revealing additional bullet points that each is benefit rich in its own right. It's like "but wait, there's more!"

(Yes, I hate informercials too, but there's a reason why they keep running the darned things: the formula works.)

As mentioned above, it's important to note that every block of text on every bullet point is revealed one at a time and you never want the Audience to feel assaulted with a large block of text. "Progressive reveal" or the use of "animations," as they are referred to in Microsoft PowerPoint, are important so that your Audience members will take in every word that you're showing them, word for word.

Agenda item 4: Where's The Proof?

It's almost inevitable that some of the very best prospects who attend your online presentation will have purchased from your competitors in the past and that they will have had a less-than-satisfactory experience.

That being the case, most of your best attendees are going to be skeptical.

You simply cannot expect for them to take your word for it, that you are good at what you do.

You must provide them with evidence that removes any reasonable doubt from their mind regarding the fact that you can deliver on the promise that's inherent in the title slide.

The best proof is visual and objective.

Numbers.

Metrics.

Photos.

Copies.

Inarguable facts.

For example, how much weight did your last three weight-loss clients lose on average?

Can you demonstrate that with "before and after" photos?

Or show me the before and after Key Performance Indicator dashboards from your last three clients who hired you to increase the engagement and productivity levels of their team members.

In my case, I show screenshots that are copies of both webinar numbers, my booking system showing the number of inbound, new client inquiry bookings that have been made, as well as a separate screenshot showing the volume of new sales, taken from our online shopping cart.

If you don't have objective numbers or images as proof, then use the next best thing, which is what I call the "Sam and

Pam" scenario and reword the agenda item to "What's The Transformation?"

In this refinement of "The Proof," you show a picture of "Sam" who is a fictitious but typical *"before"* client scenario and all of his related pain and frustration.

In other words. you paint the picture of your Audience members in terms of what they are currently suffering because they don't have your solution implemented into their business or life.

Then you switch to the "Pam" slide, showing an equally fictitious but also equally typical client *after* they finished working with you, and you describe the opposite of the symptoms and related pain and frustration that you articulated when you are talking about Sam.

This before and after scenario of fictitious but typical pre- and post-client examples are not as powerful as metric, objective images, but they still work pretty darned well.

Here are my "Where's The Proof" slide:

Firstly, here are the slides showing the numbers booked for my webinars.

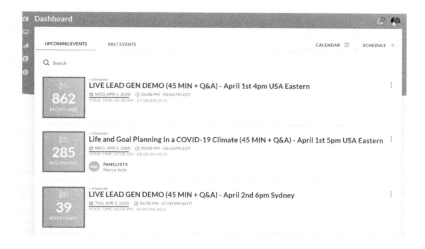

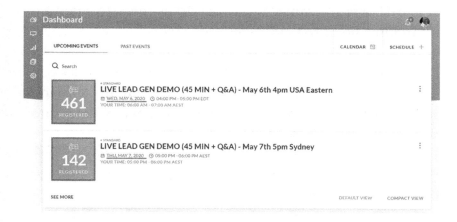

Second up is the slide that shows that I generated 72 new client inquiry bookings over a 90 day period, which is more than one highly qualified new client inquiry, every business day.

And thirdly, I flash the slide showing sales from our shopping cart over the same 90-day period as the above new client inquiry bookings slide covered.

This takes all of 5 seconds because for me, it's the icky bit (like a "financial selfie") and besides, that's all my Audience needs to gain the impression that I can generate the sort of revenue that they'd like to enjoy too.

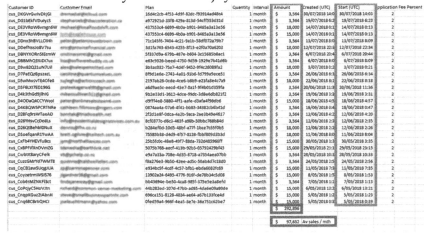

Finally, under the same agenda item, is the coup de grâce.

This is where you can have your Audience's motivation piqued because you've just showed them the sort of results they will want, and with the next slide they will feel that it gets even better because they don't have to do the things that they don't want to do in order to get those sort of results.

I call this "stacking" because I stack layer upon layer of "it gets even better."

And then, I switch it up by providing a stark contrast to all the things they mercifully don't have to do and that they don't want to do with something they instinctively feel would be easy to do.

And remember, while these are my slides, the same princi-ples and the same sequence applies to creating a powerfully persuasive presentation.

Agenda item 5: The Three Principles

The Three Principles are a key part of any Persuasion Se-quence, be they embedded in a book or marketing webinar.

What we are looking to achieve here is to create a series of "light bulb" moments where you take your Audience from not knowing a thing, to suddenly appreciating the truth of that same thing.

We achieve this in a way that is analogous to having them sitting in a dark room and then turning the light on.

By creating these lightbulb moments, your credibility as the person who can lead them out of their ignorance and "dark-ness," and toward the promised benefit-rich land of their desires is significantly enhanced.

In addition to that, this agenda item is designed to set your Audience up for the next section which is "The Demonstration" of how you work with your clients, by highlighting the foundational principles that explain why your methodology is so effective.

In my online presentation, I precede my demonstration that includes "the best Audience, the best Asset, and the best call to Action" (see below), with The Three Principles, just as I have done in this book.

It's worth repeating that I share The Three Principles so that when I cover The Demonstration (of my method) in the next agenda item, my attendees' perception of the effectiveness of my method is dramatically enhanced because I'm actually bringing those three principles to life in the Demonstration of my methodology.

The principles are initially presented deliberately as a metaphor or an analogy and as such are designed to be cryptic and not easily understood.

That's the equivalent of having my Audience sitting in the dark. When I tell them the Key Principles, they won't understand what I mean.

For example, instead of talking about "avoiding Hugh Jackman marketing," I could simply say that you need to create an opportunity for prospects to get to know you before you present them with the idea of talking about working together. But if I explained the principle that way, there would be no lightbulb moment.

It would be simply stating what many people believe they already know, even though they may not be currently practicing it.

Your Key Principles must therefore be presented in a way that's cryptic, otherwise your attendees don't have the experience of metaphorically sitting in the dark and having you turn the light on.

It's just not as enlightening otherwise (pardon my pun).

Never underestimate the importance of preparing your attendees' minds prior to leading them through the Demonstration agenda section where you show them "how it all works."

It takes me a solid 25 minutes to get to The Demonstration part of my agenda.

Contrast that to many presenters who fail to till the ground of their Audiences' minds before they sow their seeds.

And at the risk of plagiarizing a quite well-known spiritual teacher, the seeds that fall on the hard and closed ground of the mind will never take root and grow.

Here are the slides from the Three Principles part of my presentation.

The Three Immutable Elements of Marketing the Invisible (MTI)

1 You are not Hugh Jackman

2 Every day you do what you want

3 Never outsource your oxygen

The next slide is where I tell the story of asking my wife what she would say if Hugh Jackman knocked on our front door and proposed marriage to her (fortunately he has not done so yet).

You are not Hugh Jackman.

And this next slide is where I explain that dogs want to bark and cats want to meow and that 97% of marketing efforts failed for one simple reason, which is people are trying to do something that they don't want to do.

I explain that if you don't want to set up complicated online funnels (see above), then either you'll never start or you'll start and stop or at best you'll do it very poorly. Just like a dog that is trying to meow.

Every day you do what you want to do.

And the third principle is to never outsource your oxygen supply.

With this one, I'm explaining that they should not simply outsource their lead generation to an agency. I explain that new client inquiries to a business are like oxygen to a body. If you don't have enough, then there's a death.

In the former instance, the death is of a business and it's slow, and in the latter instance the death is of a body and it's breathtakingly fast (again, apologies for the pun).

I go on to explain that only one out of ten marketing agencies, at best, are any good at what they do and that the rest will simply take your money for between three and six months until you realize that you're not getting a return on that money.

Then you cancel with a polite email telling them that you're just taking a break and that you will circle back at another time when you're not quite so busy.

I go on to explain to my Audience that even if they are fortunate enough to find the one in ten agencies that generates a return on the investment for their fees, they should firstly write me an email to let me know who they are because I'll hire them. I'll advise them to keep working with that agency but limit their supply to no more than 33% of total new client inquiries.

Otherwise you end up with a dependency on them just like you've outsourced your oxygen supply.

Should the supply fail for any reason, then you're in trouble.

Never outsource your oxygen supply.

Note that the Three Principles are a prime opportunity, not only to create light bulb moments for your Audience but, along with the "Without" section described above, they also give you the opportunity to ethically and logically cut off what your Audience might perceive to be options other than working with you.

That little tip, on its own, is gold. Re-reading of the previous paragraph is highly recommended.

Agenda item 6: The Demonstration

The Demonstration is the part of your presentation where you answer the question that Audience members will have in their minds in regard to your service: *"how does it all work?"*

And by the end of this section, you want them to think *"Ah yes, I can see how that would work very well,"* in respect to whatever the promise was inherent in your title.

So far, your presentation has provided proof that you are capable of delivering on the promise you've made in your title.

We've also motivated the Audience with your promise.

And we've provided evidence of how well your service works, and we've built a platform (The Three Principles) to validate the effectiveness of your methodology.

We've ethically motivated your Audience members and brought them to a point where they want to know how you work with your clients.

As mentioned above (it's worth repeating), when the Audience completes The Demonstration part of your online presentation, you want them thinking, *"yes, this makes sense; I can see how it would work very well."*

A lot of marketers argue that people buy based on emotion and justify their purchase afterward with logic.

That's only true in some situations.

If your Audience is comprised of sophisticated buyers who have a lot of experience, then they will want to justify their purchase *before* they hand over their money.

We therefore need to make sure that The Demonstration confirms that the way you work with your clients will result in the transformation that you have promised your Audience in your title slide.

And remember my maxim: *"complication destroys motivation."* Keep your explanation of how you work with your clients very simple.

Try to stick to three parts.

Your Audience only needs to be convinced that you can deliver on the promise in your title.

Any content after you have established your capability is superfluous and runs the risk of confusing you and thereby lowering your motivation levels.

If, like me, you have a model that includes more than three parts, choose to either reformat it into a three-part model, as I have done, or tell your Audience that you don't have enough time to cover the whole model and that you're going to feature three parts which will provide them with the most value in the time that you have.

Then pick the three parts that do the best job of demonstrating how you bring to life The Three Principles in your model so that you validate how effective your method is.

This slide is where I explain why webinars are the ultimate marketing Asset.

✔ Avoids Hugh Jackman marketing
✔ Taps into "want to" not "should do"
✔ Has you in charge of the lead supply
✔ Time and cost efficient
✔ Global reach
✔ Webcams on increases engagement
✔ 100% trackable leads
✔ Pre event reminds 100% automated
✔ Post event follow up 100% automated

I follow that up with a series of slides which reveal OPN (see Chapter Two) as being the ultimate source of Audiences because it is free and of relatively high quality and the source is inexhaustible.

I repeat my assertion that webinars offer a combination of optimal efficiency and effectiveness (that's represented by the image in the middle below) and that the best call to Action in most cases is the opportunity for people to book a time to talk with you and see if you have something that's going to be a fit for their needs (represented by the blue banner in the image below).

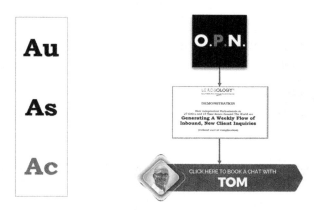

Agenda item 7: Want to Implement This?

There are two parts to this agenda item.

The first part includes a simple slide of the key features of how I work with clients.

In my case, that includes the fact that we have an **online program** (this is the first feature) where clients can access and implement our lead generation system (Audience, Asset and Action) at their own pace.

On the same slide, I highlight our weekly online **Implementation Support Sessions** (second feature) in the form of small group webinar meetings where my co-coach and I can help to make the implementation of the online modules faster and simpler and easier and more effective.

WHAT is the outcome?

You wake up every Monday morning and while sipping your coffee, you open your calendar and you feel a smile spread across your face as you see bookings from prospective Ideal Clients who want to know more about working with you and...

✓ Inbound

✓ Know your fee range

✓ Timing is good

✓ Know how you work

✓ Hope to confirm you have what they need

WHAT do we implement?

1 AUDIENCE
1. 12 point ID criteria
2. 2 step engagement
3. 3 step conversion
4. Prius strategy
5. Psych. reciprocity
6. Godfather offer

2 ASSET
1. Demonstration
2. Motivation
3. Qualification
4. Differentiation
5. Elimination
6. Education
7. Evidence
8. Offer

3 ACTION
1. Motivation
2. Filters
3. Pre-education
4. Conversion
5. Risk reversal
6. Options
7. MD Consult

HOW are we implementing?

27 Modules
at your own pace

24/7 Client
Community Center

3 Live Weekly
Support Sessions

And on that slide, I also mention our **Client Communication Center** (third feature) where our clients can direct-message my support team and me with questions in between the live Implementation Support Sessions.

You need to keep this part of your presentation very simple.

For me, those three features mentioned above are presented on one slide and I move through them quickly.

Extra detail belongs on your website's sales page (e.g. **www. iWantSolo.com)** which you can direct people to at the end of the webinar if you are offering for people to sign up directly to become a client, as opposed to you offering them a conversation to explore working together. I'll cover both options in the next chapter.

The second part of this agenda item is your Call to Action.

What does an attendee need to do in order to take the next step toward working with you?

What you need to know to move forward

✓ Leadsology® is <u>not</u> a training program

✓ Leadsology® <u>is</u> a done-with-you implementation program

✓ 8 weeks to implement at 8 hours a week – the leads flow after that

✓ Starts @ US$495/month over 12 months with 12 months support

www.BookAChatWithTom.com

When you give your Audiences your Call to Action, you will generate a lot more inquiries if you talk to the elephant in the room.

Every industry has one.

It's the negative past experience that your Audience will have endured when dealing with your competitors that prevents them from moving forward with you, unless you clear their concern out of their mind.

Let's say you are selling heavy machinery.

Maybe your Audiences has had a common experience of poor after-sales service. If that's the case, you need to come up with a strategy to mitigate them feeling that they might experience the same problem again.

Or let's say you're offering corporate training.

But maybe your Audiences has had a common experience of hiring trainers in the past and getting all excited, but after the training was done, maybe three months later, none of it seemed to stick.

Or perhaps you are marketing a program which shows your clients how to develop their own online course so they can scale in regard to how many people they serve as well as their own revenue.

But maybe a common experience amongst your Audience is that they had enrolled in something similar before, but failed to implement. In that case, failure to implement is the elephant in the room that you need to address with a strategy so that your Audience feels confident that won't happen again.

In my industry, the elephant in the room is simple.

The majority of my clients tell me that they previously paid good money to someone who said something like "trust me, give me your money and I'll show you how to get new clients on board."

Around three months after the money was handed over however, all my client had to show for that transaction was an empty bank account balance. The new clients were definitely not flowing in the door as promised.

When I discovered that the majority of my new clients had given money to people like that, not just once or twice or even three times but more often seven or even nine times, I knew I had to speak to that particular elephant in the room.

The way I address it is to offer a 30-day free test drive of my program.

(I don't offer this to private clients because there's a lot more work upfront for me with them).

For those clients whom my program is a fit for, I offer 30 days of working together because it mitigates the risk they feel in regard to repeating their experience of giving money to people who say "trust me, give me money and I'll show you how to get new clients on board."

My famous No-Brainer "Godfather" Offer

✓ Benefit from full access and work with me to implement for 30 days

✓ If for ANY reason you want to cancel, you pay nothing (no questions)

✓ Launch in less than 90 days and you only fund 2 payments

✓ JVs with Leadsology® clients can easily pay for your fees and more

✓ Question: given that this program pays for itself, is there any reason why you would NOT want this?

www.BookAChatWithTom.com

When people find out about my free 30-day test drive offer, the most common question I get asked is about people ripping me off.

I understand why they would ask that question because I promise (and deliver) 30 days of unfettered access to all of the intellectual property that I've developed for my Audience, Asset and Action model that can bring in a weekly flow of high-quality, inbound, new client inquiries for the rest of their lives.

I literally give them access to all 51 modules that I've developed over 11 years and that I paid over $100,000 to instructional designers to put online and make them easy for my clients to follow.

Not only do I give each new client full access to all of that intellectual property, without charging them a cent, I also show up to multiple small-group zoom calls each week to answer questions and help my clients implement what they been learning when they're working through the 51 modules.

And if that's not enough, I also give them 24/7 messaging access in our Client Communication Center for which we use www.slack.com so we can keep in touch between the live support sessions.

At this point, I feel like saying "but wait there's more" and at the risk of sounding like a tacky infomercial, there is more.

Every new client gets my mobile phone number for them to use if they ever feel stuck or neglected and not getting answers to the questions they have.

And when I give it to them, I tell them I'm happy for them to have it because the support that we offer is better than I've seen anywhere in the entire world for our type of program, and that I therefore have a high degree of confidence that they will never need to call me.

Remember: all of this is given without them paying me even one brass cent.

In the interest of full and open disclosure however, when the new client enrolls in my program, they submit their credit card and digitally sign a set of simple and clear conditions, one of which is that we will be debiting their card after 30 days unless they cancel.

But we make it easy for them to cancel by providing them with a copy of their agreement along with the email address to use if they choose to cancel.

So now, back to the question that I receive regularly as to how much I get ripped off due to offering something that is so generous.

Before I answer it however, I first of all want to reinforce the point that it's critical if you want to maximize your webinar marketing results to speak to whatever elephant is in the room in your Audience's minds.

I must confess that I was pretty nervous when I first introduced my 30-day free test drive offer.

But to my relief, I found that a large majority of people have integrity and don't rip me off.

I would say it's less than one out of every 50 new clients who, as best I can tell, have deliberately enrolled, downloaded everything and then canceled their subscription within a day or two.

And I'm prepared to pay that price because it brings in so many more new clients than would be the case if I didn't make that offer.

And around one in 20 will cancel after two or three weeks and normally they provide what appears to be a valid reason, even though I am quite explicit that I don't require a reason and won't ask them for one.

The question remains however: why aren't more people ripping me off?

And the answer once again comes back to context.

To become a new client, a prospect has to pass through many filters. Eight filters in fact.

And just like a water filter, every filter improves the "purity" of my prospects.

The first filter is that the new client who has accepted my 30-day free test drive was subscribed to someone else's email list, and that someone else became an OPN Partner and kindly promoted my webinar.

Filter number two is that it's very likely that person had stayed subscribed to my OPN Partner's email list for some length of time, probably a period of some years, in order to be still subscribed at the time that my OPN Partner sent out the offer to attend my webinar.

Filter number three is that they received the email invitation from my OPN Partner to attend my webinar and they not only read that email, but they also clicked on the link and registered for my webinar.

Filter number four is that they showed up to the webinar. The exception are those new client inquiries that come from the follow-up sequence.

Filter number five is that they stayed to the end of the webinar, which is where I revealed the Call to Action, being to go ahead and book a consult so we could talk about whether I have something that might fit their lead generation needs.

Filter number six is that they responded to that Call to Action and booked a time to talk with me.

Filter number seven is that they showed up to that meeting.

Filter number eight is that they pulled out the credit card at the program enrollment page and entered their details and signed the agreement.

So that's the context for the offer and acceptance of my 30-day free test drive: eight quality-control filters.

By contrast, if I had advertised on say Facebook or some other social media platform with the same Call to Action, I have no doubt that I would be flooded with rip-off artists.

I offer that explanation for three reasons.

Firstly, because having heard about my test drive offer you are probably one of the ones who would be wondering about how it is I don't simply get ripped off.

Secondly, and even more importantly, is to encourage you to come up with your own risk mitigation offer that addresses the elephant in the room of your Audiences by reason of the common negative experiences that many of them will have had when dealing with your inferior competitors in the past.

Thirdly, you may wish to consider popping over to www. iWantSolo.com and signing up for the 30-day free test drive.

I mean, why would you not do that?

And that's the response you need to strive to achieve for your Audience — that they can't think of a reason not to move ahead with you at every stage of the marketing and buying process.

Agenda item 8: Questions and Answers

Most of your attendees won't ask questions.

140 | TOM POLAND

And the ones who do will typically ask a lot of questions.

It seems that these are the two types of people who attend online presentations: those who don't ask questions and those who ask a lot of questions. The latter are a small minority.

So, you'll need to moderate the Q&A to make sure that a small number of people are not hogging the time.

One way to get the ball rolling so that those people who are more reluctant to ask questions start to feel engaged, is to have two or three sample questions that you trot out at the start of the Q&A.

Typically, what I'll say is something like this *"while you're thinking of questions you might like to ask, let me just give you a couple of the questions that normally come up and my responses."*

Then I can ask questions about whether there is a money-back guarantee, or what level of technical expertise is required, or if this works for people in retail and so on.

Note that while you are covering the Q&A, you should keep your Call To Action slide visible on the screen, which may include a link for people to reach out and book a time to talk with you (e.g. www.BookAChatWithTom.com), or it may include a link for them to go ahead and enroll in your program (e.g. www.iWantSolo.com).

Either way, keep that Call To Action slide visible during the Q&A so that people know how to take action.

CHAPTER FOUR

Enhancing Captivation

THERE ARE A bunch of ways, in addition to the methods recommended in the last chapter, of captivating your Audience's attention. Here are some of my favorites.

OPEN LOOPS

In the same way that a lot of phrases or terms in the English language take on new meaning over time, the definition of an Open Loop was originally "a control system in which an input alters the output but the output has no feedback loop and therefore no effect on the input."

This is one instance where I'm more than happy that the definition has morphed to include something other than was originally intended.

In webinar terms and in presentations generally, an "Open Loop" refers to something that's incomplete or unfinished.

The beauty of the Open Loop is that it stimulates an inherent compulsion that we humans have for finishing a thing.

For example, some people would get quite frustrated that if I didn't finish this...

...sentence.

Or imagine for example, you are mowing your lawn and the gas ran out just as you were turning to finish the last strip of lawn.

That would be frustrating, right?

In much the same way as you would desperately want to mow down that last row of grass, your Audience members will want to finish the things that you start.

Imagine you attended a presentation and you are handed some pages of notes and the presenter started working his or her way through the notes in sequence and then you came across this part:

The three essential ingredients for maximizing response rates on webinars:

1. 1. Captivation using stories, metaphors, and analogies.

2. 2. Demonstration of your professional capabilities.

3. 3. C............ T....... A.............

Notice how I only gave you the first initial of the three words in bullet point number three?

To put you out of your misery. those three words are:

"Call To Action."

There now. Feel better?

Of course you do. If you are like 99.9% of the other human beings on this planet. you have a strong urge for what psychologists call "closure."

We hate uncertainty.

In fact, psychologists tell us that we would rather be told bad health news, even if that news indicates we're dying, than to remain in the dark about what the illness or condition is.

Smart presenters ethically exploit this need for closure by presenting Open Loops during the presentation.

THE POWER OF VISUAL MODELS

A Visual Model is a graphic that visually explains a concept that could otherwise be explained with words. Often, a Visual Model can explain a complicated concept much easier and faster and more effectively than a whole bunch of words.

For example, when I wanted to bring to life the concept of how to create a life of conscious choice, I created a visual model that I called a "Life Planning Pyramid."

It took the shape of a pyramid, obviously, and the base of the pyramid represented Values and on top of that was Vision and on top of that was Goals and the peak of the pyramid represented Actions.

By visually showing a pyramid and then by filling in the label for each section of the pyramid from bottom to top (Values, Vision, Goals and Action), I could progressively reveal the whole model and the same time keep my Audience engaged by using the Open Loop device mentioned above combined with a Visual Model.

Open Loops and Visual Models combined are a powerfully engaging "one-two" punch.

By contrast, I could have simply given my Audience a bunch of bullet points with the relevant text (Values, Vision, Goals, Action), but I would have failed to maximize the opportunity for Captivation.

Visual Models are particularly useful in presentations when you want to convey the impression that you have something proprietary.

When I wrote my first book on inbound lead generation, I created the "Leadsology® Model" which included ten parts including:

1. Magic

2. Market

3. Message

4. Medium

5. Model

6. Marketing

7. Measures

8. Style

9. Scale

10. Structure

You can reference the model here **https://www.leadsology. guru/the-model/** to see how it looks visually.

The thing about my method is that it's unique.

But if I fail to express that uniqueness in a manner that is differentiated, then I fail to allow people to match their perception with the reality that what I've got is different.

Not only does the model allow you to convey to your Audiences that you have something that is unique, it also allows you to demonstrate to them how you work with your clients and why your method, as embodied by your Visual Model, works so well.

Visual Models also allow you to demonstrate a logical sequence in how you work with your clients.

Simply and elegantly and powerfully.

The ten words that I've listed above are by no means unique.

But the sequence is.

And it's the sequence that allows Audiences to understand that there is a logic to your methodology, and furthermore it allows them to realize that what you've got works darned well.

Additionally, by representing your methods visually, it is often possible to take what would otherwise be a complicated explanation and make it understood much faster by a larger percentage of your Audience.

If complication is the enemy of motivation, then simplicity is the friend of sales.

The final word on developing a Visual Model (or Visual Models) to represent how you work with your client, is that they stimulate a high level of intrigue and curiosity in Audiences.

And that of course in turn increases captivation which in turn enhances the rather satisfying experience of seeing more cash flowing into your bank account.

THE CONCEPT CONVEYOR

How do you convey an idea across the gap between your mind to the minds of your Audience members?

And probably more importantly, how to you get that idea across in a way that is clear, captivating, and memorable?

That's the purpose I developed The Concept Conveyor for, so that you can do what many of the great speakers do, which is to convey an idea with clarity and captivation and leave that concept as a mental footprint in the minds of your Audiences.

Of course, you can simply tell an Audience what you want to say.

But that is not especially captivating, and neither is it especially memorable.

Instead, use The Concept Conveyor to captivate and educate your Audience on the key concepts you want to communicate. Here's the formula.

1. Give the concept a label.

2. Explain the idea.

3. Express the idea as a metaphor, simile, analogy, or story.

4. Give an example.

5. Finish with a recommendation.

The great communicators use these elements or parts of them, all the time.

You come away from their talks feeling illuminated, empowered, and motivated and more than likely you are so energized by their words that you share some of the highlights with your friends.

And maybe, you sometimes wistfully wonder how you could captivate and illuminate Audiences in the same way.

Well, in a moment, you'll know exactly how to do that.

The Concept Conveyor is like watching a magic show with Penn and Teller where they saw a body in half or have a hundred doves fly out of one white silk glove.

It's wonderful and mesmerizing but you have no idea how they do it until ... they take you backstage and show you the illusions created by their props and sleight of hand.

Then you think "heck, with a bit of practice, I could do that!"

And so it is with The Concept Conveyor.

I'm now going to take you backstage, and show you how it's done.

And then my strongest recommendation is that you use the five steps of The Concept Conveyor like a recipe whenever you want to convey a concept in a memorable, clear, and captivating manner.

At this point please push the pause button in your brain.

Have you noticed what I've done so far?

I have:

1. Given the concept a label. In this case the label is The Concept Conveyor.

2. Explained the idea.

3. Expressed the idea as a simile (it's like Penn and Teller explaining a magic trick).

4. Given an example (this whole section is an example of itself).

5. Finished with a recommendation (use this formula in your next presentation).

See how easy that was?

By the way, any time you give something a label, it suddenly becomes more authoritative when you put the word "The" in front of it.

The thing you are talking about is suddenly no longer "a," meaning one of potentially many, but rather it's "The," as in the only one.

And as such it suddenly carries more authority.

Now that you know about The Concept Conveyor, your eyes will be opened to the fact that I use that precise recipe all throughout all my books and webinars.

Witness:

"The Four Levels Of Psychological Allure"

"The Three Principles"

"The Wedge"

"The Spiral"

"The SEW Segmentation Formula"

"Sophie's Choice"

"The Circle of Sequels"

"The Black Jellybean"

"The Persuasion Sequence"

"The Beachhead"

"Hugh Jackman Marketing"

... just to name a few.

THE DECLARATION

(Yep, I'm about to use The Concept Conveyor again.)

This technique drops a thought into the minds of your Audience in the form of a declaration of truth, and it does so in such a way that many in your Audience reach for a pen and start writing down what you just said.

And afterward, they will quote you on it.

The Declaration is one of those show-stopping moments where people pause and ponder. It's the mental equivalent of a fireworks display lighting up the night sky, which has everyone gazing in the direction you are pointing toward.

Here are some examples, many that I've used in this very book:

"Never outsource your oxygen supply."

"Selling is what you have to do when your marketing sucks."

"If it's not captivating, it's not marketing."

"There is an old saying that nothing happens in a business until something is sold. That's true. But nothing gets sold until a lead is generated."

"Build your email list around your strategy, not your strategy around your email list"

"Mastery is simple: just do a thing one million times."

"The enemy of motivation is complication."

The Declaration is tougher to create than The Concept Conveyor, but what you'll find is that, unlike the latter, which can be constructed step-by-step, Declarations will come to you as you are speaking or writing or contemplating an idea.

I mean that literally: *Declarations will come to you.*

Maybe they come from your unconscious or the superconscious or from a fairy or a pixie or an alien. God only know where they come from; I certainly don't.

But what I do know, and with great certainty, is that they come to you as you seek to master a point you want to make by thinking about that point, day in and day out, over weeks and months and sometimes years.

As my Little Bavarian Bulldozer (German wife) once told me: "Übung macht den Meister" or "Practice makes the Master." Do a thing often enough and The Declarations will come.

Pitch, Pause and Pace

Simply put, you want to vary the pitch of your voice, vary the pace of your delivery and occasionally pause for ... dramatic effect.

A top tip is to listen to news readers who are mostly consummate professionals at Pitch, Pause, and Pace. That's not to say you should deliver your presentation sounding like Walter Cronkite or Barbara Walters (oops, am I showing my age now?), but rather that you should use the same principles of Pitch, Pause, and Pace to make your own style of presenting more engaging to your Audience.

The best time and day to run webinars

One of the most frequent questions I get asked about in regard to marketing with webinars is about the best day and time to run them.

The answer depends on the Audience.

Remember, context is everything. If your Audience is the mothers of preschool children, then you should probably run your webinars at a time when the children are likely to be in bed. Perhaps 7 p.m.

My sweet spot however is 4 p.m. on a Wednesday.

Tuesdays and Thursdays are okay too.

I've run hundreds of events, both physical and digital, pretty much at every time of the day and every day of the week that you could imagine.

But around 20 years ago, I settled on 4 p.m. on Wednesday as being best.

I can't definitively tell you *why* it's the best time, but I can tell you that for a short event targeting a business Audience, it *is* the best.

Over the course of those hundreds of events, I had measured the number of registrants and attendees and inquiries and sales on virtually every occasion.

I tested breakfast meetings, lunch meetings, evening meetings and pretty much everything in between.

When I ran marketing *seminars* where people attended physically (yesterday's equivalent of a marketing *webinar*) where there was no charge for the event, we typically had 67% of registrants turn up.

When I started running marketing webinars back in 2008, we typically had 40% of registrants turn up. That dropped later on, and I'll explain why and what I did about it in Chapter Five.

But in the meantime, just know that 4 p.m. on Wednesday worked very well for me when I was running physical seminars as well as it does now, running digital webinars.

When I ran physical seminars, we would hire a conference room in the center of a city which was population-dense in terms of our ideal clients.

They'd be able to get to the conference center by 4 p.m. before peak-hour traffic caused delays, and they could leave the seminar after the bulk of peak traffic had eased, then still be home for a late dinner with their family.

Maybe that's why that time worked so well, but I care less about why and more about the fact that it worked best.

My primary target market is North America but I live on the East Coast and Australia.

And because I don't like to get out of bed earlier than I really have to, I tested running webinars at 4 p.m. US Eastern (6 a.m. my time here in little Castaways Beach) and 5 p.m. and 6 p.m. and 7 p.m.

In particular, I was hoping that the 7 p.m. webinar would prove to be the most profitable because that would allow me to start at "gentleman's hours" here, being 9 a.m.

Sadly, it was not to be.

These days, we average a 41% attendance rate at 4 p.m. US Eastern. And every hour later that I start the webinar, attendance rates drop until I get 28% at 7 p.m.

Sleeping in costs me a lot of money and I don't like that idea, so when I run my monthly webinar, I get my butt out of bed at 5 a.m., jump in the swimming pool and then make myself a double shot of espresso so my adrenals can kickstart my brain and other vital organs.

I'm told that I'm not fun to be with in the mornings, before the caffeine has kicked in.

In fact, when my wife once complained about my early morning Neanderthal-like grunting, I informed her that I was not responsible for the quality of my responses if she chose to ask me questions before I had my coffee.

But back to the point at hand.

If I was living in the United States, then I could probably run webinars anytime between 1 p.m. Eastern (10 a.m. Pacific) and 4 p.m. Eastern (1 p.m. Pacific) because that comfortably straddles the four time zones across North America and that timing embraces business hours, which is when my ideal clients prefer to attend webinars.

Unless you are targeting people who have a day job, in which case you want to try running evening webinars, you'll find too much competition when you run webinars in the evening.

Think about it.

Let's say you register for my webinar and I foolishly promoted in an 8 p.m. start time.

You get home from work after a busy day and you sit down and maybe play with the kids and then have dinner with them over a couple of glasses of relaxing wine or whiskey.

While still sipping on your favorite beverage, you do the right thing and read your kids a bedtime story and tuck them into bed. You walk back to the kitchen and pour yourself "just one more."

Meantime, your wife/husband/boyfriend/girlfriend/whatever has turned Netflix on and is chuckling away at the jokes of a stand-up comedian who is among the best of the best.

You look at the television, you look at the glass in your hand, you see your comfortable and inviting recliner sitting empty waiting for you, and then you realize that it's only two minutes to the start of my webinar.

What are you going to do?

Hell, if that were me and I was also presenting, I'd be sorely tempted to not turn up to my own webinar!

Of course I *would* show up and present, but I'm sure you get my point, which is that if your prospect has endured a long day at work it's going be tough for you to compete against a half decent Cabernet Sauvignon and Netflix.

In the interests of full disclosure, I also run another webinar at 3 a.m. US Eastern.

That's because I have a global Audience and I want to offer a convenient time for my British and European friends as well as my Australian and New Zealand friends.

At 3 a.m. US Eastern, it's 5 p.m. here on the East Coast of Australia and 7 p.m. in New Zealand (an incredible little country that punches far above its weight in terms of professional development), 9 a.m. in Germany and 8 a.m. in the United Kingdom.

By running my webinars once a month at 6 a.m., and 5 p.m. my time, I cover almost the entire planet in a total of two hours. If you're only targeting an Audience across a handful of time zones, then you don't need to run webinars every time you present.

Evergreen versus live webinars

Another common question that I get asked is whether to make the webinars live or what is generally referred to as evergreen.

The term "live" clearly means exactly what it suggests which is that you run your webinar in real time and the Audiences is there at the same time. Nothing is pre-recorded and it's just like you are on a stage with a physical Audience at a conference center. If you sneeze, they hear it. If you "um" and "er," they hear that too. With live, what you do is what they get.

By contrast, "evergreen" means that you're not there and typically that the Audience can start their attendance when they prefer, which may be from a selection of start times including "watch yesterday's replay now."

With the advent of evergreen webinars some 10 years ago, many marketers set them up and tried to pretend that they were live.

There's plenty of platforms that will include features such as a fake attendees list, fake questions, and so on. With these platforms, it appears that the presenter is presenting live when in fact he or she is probably sitting by the swimming pool sipping a Pina Colada.

That said, we still have the question of live versus evergreen. Which one is better?

If you're selling one-dollar lollipops to school kids, then by all means run an evergreen webinar.

However, if you're selling $500,000 luxury vehicles to the rich and famous, then I would recommend you show up live.

For the most part, I still run live webinars every month for the following reasons.

Reason #1: Unless you are explicit about the fact that the webinar is pre-recorded, you open yourself up to accusations (justified) of being less than transparent and a prospect is legitimately entitled to ask, will the transparency improve once they hand over their money. And the answer they will give themselves is "probably not."

Reason #2: The above means that, if you are going to run an evergreen webinar, in the interest of sending the message that you aren't trying to make it out to be something that it's not (live), it pays, to be explicit that it is pre-recorded. The problem with such a declaration is that your engagement levels are going to go to hell in a handbasket. The Audience member will clear emails, check their Facebook feed, and maybe surf YouTube. Who knows? They know that you couldn't be bothered to show up, so why should they?

Reason #3: And that leads neatly into the third challenge with evergreen, which is that you are in danger of sending the message that you are disengaging with your Audience for reasons of laziness or simply not caring enough to show up live. Either way, it's not a message I want to send to my Audiences.

Reason #4: For me, it's about mastery. I have an innate and completely non-optional need to get better and better at what I do for a profession. And the only way I can improve is to avoid the temptation of offering prerecorded webinars which circumvent the need to run them live. The reason is simple: if I want mastery then I need to run 10,000 live webinars, not 10,000 replays.

Note that none of the above reasons should bother you if you are marketing a relatively low-cost product or service where your Audience will be happy to simply pull out their credit card, buy what you are offering, and have no need for input/advice/support from you after they have purchased.

A bit earlier, I wrote about the challenge of increasing captivation levels.

When I run a Boardroom Briefing where I have a small group of attendees of perhaps six or eight and the WebCams are on, the percentage of inquiries increases more than three times. And that's because captivation levels are higher.

With traditional live webinars, captivation levels are lower but you have large numbers, which compensates for the smaller percentage of people who will reach out to you by the end of your webinar, when compared to Boardroom Briefings.

That lower captivation level, and therefore lower engagement level and therefore low response level, gets even worse when you run evergreen webinars.

But if you have the volume and you don't have the time, then evergreen webinars make perfect sense, once you have mastered the presentation.

On the subject of mastery, allow me to share another short story. The story goes that the famous golfer Arnold Palmer was practicing his chipping at a dedicated practice hole that was in addition to the standard 18-hole golf course.

He chipped ball after ball with many getting in the hole or close to it, with his caddie constantly clearing the balls out of the way in advance of the next ball to be chipped.

The story goes that a man was sitting close by enjoying a drink in the sun watching Arnold Palmer and became increasingly astonished at his accuracy rate.

Approaching Palmer, he introduced himself and apologized for the interruption and then said that he would give anything to be able to chip like Arnie.

Arnold looked surprised and turned to him and said "if you're that keen then I'm happy to share with you the secret of chipping so accurately." The man responded with glee and said he'd love to learn from a master like Arnold Palmer. Arnold said "it's simple, just go and chip one million balls and then you will be as accurate as I am."

How do you get better at a thing? Simple: do it one million times.

CHAPTER FIVE:

How to Filter Audiences to Generate High-quality Leads

IN CHAPTER TWO, I revealed the very best method for generating Audiences which was OPN.

That's a source of high-quality prospects that's also completely free of financial cost as well as being 100% sustainable in that you can "rinse and repeat" your presentation with a different Audience month in and month out.

In Chapter Three and Four, I revealed numerous insights that will help you make your presentation captivating and will motivate the right Audience members to want to reach out and take the next step with you.

In summary, Chapter Two covered your Audience (OPN, amongst others) and chapters 3 and 4 covered your core marketing Asset (a captivating presentation). This chapter is going to cover your call to Action.

In the world of marketing, a Call to Action is simply the explicit next step that you want a prospect to take.

And there's a whole bunch for you to choose from.

- Follow
- Connect
- Opt-in
- Subscribe
- Register
- Apply
- Read
- Listen
- View
- Join
- Click
- Call
- Email

- Book (a meeting)
- Schedule
- Ask
- Answer
- Buy
- Enroll
- Try
- Test
- Sample
- Download
- Attend
- And probably a bunch more things I haven't thought of.

Mostly though, at the end of the webinar your Call to Action is going to be for an attendee to either buy something from you or if you are a professional advisor or service provided or software developer, then that next step is probably going to be to book a time to have a conversation with you about whether the two of you should be working together.

Note To Those Marketing To Busy Executives

The following quality-filtering systems are for the small business, solopreneur, and consumer/domestic markets and are designed, in part, to keep the "tire kickers" and "idea pickers" out of your life. If, however you are targeting senior executives, there is a quality filter already innate to them which is their time.

A busy executive who books a time to talk with you for the purpose of exploring the idea of working together does not need any additional filters put in place between them and you. Their willingness to commit their time is all the indication that you need that they are likely to be serious in their intent. For the most part, executives are not going to be spending their own money with you; it will be the organization's money, so requiring them to pay a fee to meet with you is going to be counter-productive. Requiring them to fill out an extensive application form would also be counter-productive.

In the early days of developing the OPN Audience system, I delivered a presentation to 137 attendees.

I was delighted to have that many people show up to my webinar and equally excited to have 23 of them book a time to talk with me about becoming a client. I promised each person up to an hour of my time to discuss their situation and see if working together would be a good idea.

After 23 meetings, I had exactly zero new clients.

That was 23 hours of my life that were not only gone forever, but it also resulted in massive frustration and disappointment, instead of more money in my bank account balance.

Being the kindhearted person that I am, I can take some comfort in the idea that I gave 23 people insights into what I believed would be their next best steps on their journey to creating the business of their dreams.

I guess I got great karma from that, but unfortunately, I couldn't exchange that karma for groceries.

That was the day I decided I was going to put some filters in place between me and my prospects.

Allow me to illustrate what I mean with another analogy.

If I am feeling thirsty and I have no other source of water, other than a dirty pool lying in my backyard, then all is not lost.

I buy a water filter and I pump that dirty water through the filter.

If I have enough water and I have enough filters, then instead of a pool of dirty water, I have a whole bunch of bottles with pure water that will satisfy my thirst.

But that only works when I have both of the two critical elements.

The first element is a *volume* of water that is sufficient and the second is enough quality *filters* to remove the impurities in the water.

If I have the volume of water without the filters, I end up with water that undrinkable.

If I have the filters without the volume of water, I only end up with a couple of drops of drinkable water.

The volume of water is a metaphor for a significant quantity of inquiries.

The filters are a metaphor for qualifying prospects before they meet with me.

And there are a bunch of different ways to filter your inquiries so you don't end up wasting the 23 hours that I wasted.

And by the way, it's not just *my* time that I wasted.

There were 23 people who were hoping to work with me, but when they found out what I charged, decided that they couldn't afford to do so.

In case it's not already obvious, your Call to Action is pretty much the last thing that you present on your webinar.

My Call to Action is inviting people who qualify to reach out and book a time to have a conversation about whether we should be working together.

It's also valuable for you to note that I always disclose my fee range before the Call to Action.

I explain in broad terms what working together would look like alongside what that would cost my prospect. I don't want to be talking to people who can't afford to work with me.

By disclosing my minimum fee on the webinar, I save time meeting with people who can't afford to work with me and likewise they get to save their time.

I am not one for getting a whole bunch of people on a call and then twisting their arms with "seven ways to close the sale," and "when you hear the word no, it's really just a request for more information," or any other B.S. that masquerades as sales techniques.

The following are some of your better Call to Action options which incorporate qualification filters that I've alluded to above.

THE APPLICATION FORM

With this method, you direct interested attendees to your webpage form that they need to fill out, disclosing all relevant information that you need in order to assess whether they are likely to be an ideal client. That information might include the size of their business as measured by revenue or employee numbers, or it could include the geographical location and the target market or any other demographic factor or indeed psychographic factors (their motivations or reasons for wanting to meet) that might be relevant.

The application form method serves two purposes.

Firstly, it filters out the people who can't be bothered completing a form, and frankly if they can't be bothered to do that, then you don't want them as a client. Which means you also don't want to meet them for a conversation about working together. The application form is therefore a filter.

Secondly, this method helps you very quickly determine whether or not you want to meet with this person.

I've used the application form to very good effect, but when I do, I redirect the applicant immediately following the submission of their form to my online booking page.

This saves me having to reach out back to them once I receive their application because they can go ahead and book a time right away. In the unlikely event that the information contained in their application is such that I don't feel we should be working together, I email them about that and offer to cancel the meeting unless there is other information that would mean we should be meeting after all.

The Payment Option

This option normally goes with the application form option, but it adds another filter by asking prospects to pull out the credit card and make a payment in return for meeting with them.

This is a worthwhile option if you only want to speak with the best qualified prospects and you don't mind losing a few that might otherwise have become worthwhile clients.

If you are short on time and you've got more prospects than you know how to handle, then this is definitely worth considering.

When I ran this system, I made it clear on the application form page that my time was valued at $1,000 an hour and that I routinely sent invoices out at that level.

But I also offered a coupon code that reduced that amount down to just $100 for the privilege of meeting with me and having a conversation about whether or not we should be working together.

Terms and Conditions

This is the method that I finally settled on.

It bypasses the need for prospects to fill out an application form and it means that I can promote a webinar as there being "nothing to buy so leave your credit card at home."

That's important because I know an increasing number of my ideal clients are sick to death of showing up to webinars only to have some crack-addled, hyped-up, sales-clown demand that they buy before the countdown timer hits zero, but promising a free set of steak knives and other useless bonuses with every order.

The starting point for this method is the same as the others: on your Call to Action slide at the end of the presentation, you provide a brief overview of how you work with clients along with your minimum fee or your range of fees. And like the other method, you then direct interested attendees to your meeting booking page.

In this case however, the webpage is a bit longer because it explains what will happen when you meet and what will not happen and then it asks them to check several boxes to indicate that they agree with the terms and conditions for meeting.

You can check out **www.BookAChatWithTom.com** by way of example, but I can't guarantee it'll still be alive by the time you visit it.

Therefore, in case I've changed a few things or that webpage has been replaced, here's what you should put on your booking page.

Firstly, welcome your visitors and mention the fact that, if they are on the web page, then they have probably been referred by one of your clients or they may have attended one of your webinars.

Explain to them that when you meet, it won't be some sort of sales ambush but rather that it will be a conversation between two mature adults to see if you have something that would be a fit for their needs.

You can also explain to them that is not some sort of free ideas session because that wouldn't be fair to them. They might be in danger of leaving the meeting thinking that the value was in the ideas, whereas in fact it's in the implementation of the ideas, and for that they would need to be working with you.

Having explained what the meeting will not be and what it will be, you then go on to ask the prospect to agree to four conditions for meeting.

The first is that they agree that they can afford your minimum fees, which are stated explicitly at the end of your webinar again on the booking page which they are reading.

This saves you talking to people who can't afford to work with you and as mentioned previously it also saves wasting their time as well.

The second is that, when you meet and if you agree that working together is a good idea, then they already do commence within a week or two.

Otherwise, you explain, they are better to come back and book a conversation when they are closer to their anticipated start date.

This saves you getting all excited about working together only to then discover that it is not possible because they're about to embark on a three-month world trip.

If that were to happen, they would of course sincerely explain to you that they will circle back just as soon as they arrive back home, and you can be equally assured that they will not do so. People have a short attention span, and 99% of the time, you'll never hear back from them.

The third condition for meeting is that they agree that the meeting will not be some sort of sales ambush, but neither will it be some form of free ideas or brainstorming session.

The fourth condition is that they have either attended your webinar or that they commit to doing so prior to actually meeting with you. In other words, they can go ahead and book now but between the booking and the meeting they must have viewed a replay of your webinar which you will provide them a link for, in the email booking confirmation.

The reason for this last condition is that you don't want to have to explain everything to each individual over and over again.

By having them either attend your webinar live or viewing a replay, they will have the answers to 80% of the questions including how you work with your clients.

Trust me, when you generate a lot of new client inquiries, you do *not* want to be saying the same things over and over again.

You are better to spend your valuable time at your meeting with prospects focusing on their specific needs and their specific answers, as opposed to saying the same things over and over again.

And in addition to the webinar replay, I have the person who booked a time with me redirected to www.iWantSolo.com which explains in much more detail, how I work with my program clients.

CHAPTER SIX:

The Wedge. How to Maximize Attendance Rates AND Double Your Results With a Replay-Free Follow-up

IN **CHAPTER THREE,** I mentioned that if we run webinars at 4 p.m. US Eastern, then we enjoy a 41% attendance rate, relative to the number of registrants. In other words, if one hundred people register, we'll end up with around 41 of those showing up to the webinar.

That may sound like a low percentage but in the world of marketing with webinars, it's actually pretty good.

Allow me to give you a brief history of webinar attendance levels so that you will understand how powerful my promises are that are embedded in the title of this chapter.

That promise being that you can maximize attendance rates as well as doubling the response rates from each webinar by not offering a webinar replay.

That's right: do not offer a webinar replay.

Here we go with a history lesson.

In 2008 when I started running marketing with webinars, I was batting at a 40% attendance rate. That was pretty much industry-standard back then.

But a marketing colleague told me that I was leaving a lot of money on the table by not offering a replay.

So I tried it and he was right.

I typically doubled my results by offering a replay.

In terms of total sales, half would come from inquiries at the end of the webinar and the other half would come from inquiries generated by the replay video.

Nothing wrong with this picture, right?

From 2009 to 2012, the strategy of offering a video replay held up pretty darned well.

But then, being the anally retentive marketer that I am, and because I was tracking the numbers for every single darned webinar, I noticed an alarming trend.

My 40% attendance rates dropped to 35% and then dropped to 28% and then dropped to 21% and then dropped to 15% and bottomed out at 12 ½%.

I was horrified.

Every percentage point dropped was less money in my bank account.

I had colleagues who concluded that webinars were no longer profitable and who abandoned them. Many believed that we had overfished the resource.

Their Audiences couldn't be bothered with webinars anymore, they said.

The magic had disappeared, they said. And other statements, all of which painted a bleak picture for the future of marketing with webinars.

What had changed?

Having been a marketing professional for decades prior to that point, I struggled to believe that in the space of just a couple of short years, webinars had passed their use-by date.

I decided to do something radical and I made it clear in my webinar email invitations that there would be no replay under any circumstances. They either attended live or they missed out completely.

Remember: whatever result I was generating from the live webinar I was getting that same amount again with the replay.

Therefore, to cut out the replay I was potentially eliminating another 50% of my revenue and that was on top of the diminishing result I was already getting as a result of our attendance rates plummeting like the share market at the beginning of the COVID-19 pandemic.

But I figured I didn't have much to lose.

And I also had a hunch, which was that we were sending a clear and explicit message to our registrants that they needn't bother attending live because there will be a replay. In fact, at that point, replays had become ubiquitous so everyone just expected them anyhow.

But by making it clear to all and sundry that hell would freeze over before I offered a replay, my attendance rates bounced back up from the measly and unsatisfying depths of 12 ½% to 41%.

And by 2016, I was back to where I had started, in terms of attendance levels, way back in 2008.

Only now I wasn't offering a replay, and getting that 100% bump in results than I was before. And being the unreasonable bugger that I am, I missed that.

So what to do?

How would I get that extra bump after the webinar that I used to enjoy before attendance levels went to hell and a handbasket.

I knew that if I offered a replay, I would just start that darned downward attendance rate spiral again. So that option was never on the table for consideration.

So, I took another risk. That's what entrepreneurs do, right?

Bear in mind that by my own estimate, 90% of the new things that I try don't even break even. Normally they fail.

I created a follow-up sequence to my webinar that delivered the same or similar content from the webinar but not in a replay format.

I call this The Wedge, for reasons which will become obvious soon.

Here's the sequence.

Webinar Plus 60 minutes: One hour webinar

I conduct the webinar and 60 minutes later all registrants (not just attendees) receive a simple email that's very short, that thanks them for registering and offers my Call to Action, which is typically to go to my nominated webpage and a book a time to talk about becoming a client, assuming they meet the terms and conditions (see the previous chapter).

This email only goes out to registrants who did not respond to the Call to Action at the end of the webinar. In other words, it doesn't go out to someone if they've already booked a time to meet with me.

Webinar Plus One Day: Twenty-minute E-Guide

24 hours after the webinar, being a Thursday, everyone who registered to attend my webinar, and who has not responded to my Call to Action either at the end of the webinar or in the follow-up email that went out one hour afterwards, receives another email. This email confirms that I don't offer video replays but that, instead, I put together a 23-page summary of the webinar in PDF format. If they click the link, they are taken to a page where they can download that

E-Guide summary without having to opt in with their email address. I don't need their email address because they've already registered for the webinar and in doing so provided their email address.

Webinar Plus Two Days: Five-minute video

On the next day which (normally a Friday), everyone receives a third email which contains a link to a five-minute video that summarizes the content of the webinar. It's one of those videos where you see I hand sketching and writing. It's captivating. And of course, just like items one and two above, contains the Call to Action which is to book a time to have a conversation and see if I have something in my marketing arsenal that might be a fit for their lead generation needs.

Webinar Plus Three Days: One-minute blueprint

On the Saturday, a fourth email goes out offering each registrant a one-page blueprint that summarizes the content of the webinar. And again, you guessed it, the one-page blueprint contains the Call to Action. The blueprint takes around a minute to scan.

Webinar Plus Four Days: Twenty-second email

On the Sunday, those who have not yet responded receive a final email which is very short and simply advices the recipient that the opportunity to book a time to have a meeting with me is going to disappear at midnight.

So there you have it.

The webinar takes around 60 minutes and each subsequent day they receive more content that mirrors the webinar content but in different formats and with decreasing time required to consume, hence "The Wedge."

In contrast to the 60-minute webinar, the 23-page PDF takes around 20 minutes to consume, the five-minute video obviously takes only five minutes to consume, the one-page PDF takes around a minute to scan and the final email takes all of 20 seconds.

Last week, literally, I had a marketing colleague tell me that doubling our response rate from the webinar was no big deal and that I shouldn't have bothered setting up this fancy pants follow-up sequence.

I gently asked him what his attendance rates were. He told me they were 13%.

We kept the conversation going and he revealed that like me, he had previously enjoyed 40% attendance levels way back in "the good old days," but that "it was OK" because he was still doubling his results with the offer of a replay.

I'm embarrassed to admit that I felt just a tinge of satisfaction in pointing out doubling his response rate from a 13% attendance rate is not quite the same as doubling the results from a 40% attendance level.

Sure, his percentage response stayed the same, but the base number was one third as much as it used to be.

At the time of this conversation, I was on a zoom call with him with webcams on. As the math sunk in, his face slowly changed from looking relaxed to looking quizzical to looking horrified.

Poor guy. But the fact is that you can't bank a percentage; you can only bank what a client pays you.

If you follow my recommendation and make it explicit that there will be no replay for your presentation, then you will maximize your attendance levels.

If you go a step further and put into place a follow-up system, without any video replay, you'll also get to enjoy a very significant bump in your results after your presentation.

What I have just revealed to you can literally be worth millions of dollars to you. That being the case, you might want to re-read this chapter and schedule some time to start implementing.

A reminder that if you want to download copies of the three main follow-up assets I've mentioned above including the 23-page E-Guide, the five-minute video summary, and the one-page Blueprint you can do so here: **www.Marketing-WithWebinars.com/Downloads/**

Chapter Seven:

How To Choose the Style of Webinar That Is a Fit for Your Market and Your Price Point

Just to be clear, this chapter is not about the type of webinar platform that you choose, but rather the style of presentation that you choose.

Webinars are like cars in that they don't come in just one shape and size. In fact, the following gives you an insight into four distinctly different webinar styles.

Traditional Webinars

There's a pretty good chance that if you have attended webinars, they all looked pretty much the same.

A series of PowerPoint slides, some better than others, but nevertheless slide after slide with the possibility that the presenter had the webcam on and he or she was visible if you glanced up to a corner of your screen.

If that's the case, then what you experienced is a stock Traditional Webinar.

And they can work very well, but there are other options which can provide you with an even better result, provided you prepared to be a little adaptable and go out on a limb, technology wise. More on that soon.

The Traditional Webinar is best used for larger Audiences where the volume of attendees can compensate for the lower engagement levels, relative to other webinar methods I'll describe below.

The Traditional Webinar style is also perfect if you are marketing a relatively low-cost product or service. But for something at the other end of the pricing spectrum, such as high-priced consulting services or luxury goods, you may want to consider small Audience sizes so you can profit from greater engagement levels. If that sounds like a plan, please read on.

BOARDROOM BRIEFING WEBINARS

In a nutshell, these are webinars that are limited to a relatively small number of people, typically 6 to 8 attendees.

In addition to having a small Audience, attendees' webcams are automatically on, assuming they have one installed, when they enter the webinar.

Prior to the explosion in the use of Zoom meetings due to COVID-19, entering these smaller and more intimate webinars was a surprise to many people who were expecting to slip into the webinar anonymously.

Boardroom Briefings are perfect for senior executives in large organizations who tend to avoid Traditional Webinars like the plague because they associate them with B.S. marketers and don't want to subject themselves to the webinar equivalent of a hyped-up infomercial.

Part of the appeal of the Boardroom Briefing is the fact that it's going to be exclusive, relative to a Traditional Webinar.

Make sure that your invitation is explicit in pointing out that this is a smaller meeting and it is limited to only 6 to 8 attendees. Explain that you limit the numbers to ensure that every attendee can have their specific questions answered.

Boardroom Briefings are not designed for low-ticket-price items. As mentioned previously, the Traditional Webinar is best for such products and services.

That's because you are going to have much lower numbers in a Boardroom Briefing and that's fine if you have a much higher-priced product or service with bigger margins.

When that's the case, you can afford to have smaller attendee numbers because you need a lower number of conversions to justify the use of your time and the expense of the platform.

According to my records, and I've run hundreds of both traditional webinars as well as Boardroom Briefings, the smaller and more intimate and more exclusive style of webinar will convert more than three times the percentage of attendees as a traditional webinar.

But before you get too excited, remember that's three times as much of a smaller number and that's why Boardroom Briefings are best suited for higher ticket-priced services and products.

Why they convert at such a significantly higher percentage is subject to debate, but for my money, it's because of the increased engagement that comes by having your set of eyeballs connecting with their set of eyeballs.

When people are looking at you and they know that you can see them, they are much less tempted to be clearing emails or checking their Facebook feed or their LinkedIn messages during your presentation.

I once spoke to a large conference Audience in another country that has a different conference culture to anywhere else in the world that I'd spoken. As is my custom, I arrived early and sat at the back of the conference room to get a feel for the Audience and the theme of the conference.

I was horrified to see at least half the Audience were either asleep or working feverishly on their laptops. Apparently in this particular country, which shall remain nameless because of my fear of being labeled a racist, this was perfectly normal.

Speaker after speaker experienced 50% of the Audience completely ignoring them either because they were asleep or clearing emails. That's not how we behave in my country and it's probably not standard procedure for Audience members in your country either.

But my oh my, aren't I the hypocrite?

I'll pay close attention when I think the speaker can see me, but the moment my webcam is off, I will start clearing emails and tell myself that I'll keep one ear on what the presenter is saying in case they say something interesting. I've done it and maybe, just maybe, you have too?

But with Boardroom Briefings, it's different.

Your Audience see you and you see them.

Eyeballs meet eyeballs.

And so their cultural programming kicks in and they pay attention. That higher engagement level translates into higher response rates.

Therefore, if you sell high-end consulting services, luxury items, or your profit margins are nice and fat, or you are marketing to time-poor and stressed senior executives from large organizations, then consider Boardroom Briefings as a profitable alternative to traditional webinars.

Footnote: the content of your presentation won't vary one bit between a traditional webinar and a Boardroom Briefing. The only differences are that you can welcome each individual as they enter your webinar by greeting them by name (their name shows up on your attendee panel) and asking them some sort of "ice-breaker" such as the product or service they are marketing.

Touch Screen Webinars

A touch screen monitor allows you to use a stylus to draw or hand-write on the screen. Most tablets are touchscreen including iPads and Microsoft's Surface Pro laptop.

The advantage of running a Touch Screen Webinar is all about the enhanced Captivation levels that comes from hand drawing, be that in Open Loops or Visual Models or both.

The content may be the same as a Traditional Webinar or a Boardroom Briefing, but the style of presentation changes dramatically from slides to a more free-form style. Mac users can use apps like Notability for their presentations or Canva, and Windows users can use the delightfully simply Bamboo Paper from Wacom.

E-BOARD WEBINARS

In my office, I have a 75-inch Ultra High Definition (4k) interactive panel.

These devices are variously known as Smartboards (a proprietary brand name), Interactive Whiteboards, or E-Boards, which for the sake of simplicity is how I refer to them.

E-Boards have been in existence for close on 20 years but have almost exclusively been used in either corporate boardrooms or in educational institutions, be that preschool, grade school, or college and universities.

Virtually no one has used them in a marketing context. And therein lies an opportunity, for the right person and the right market.

What an Audience experiences when they attend my E-Board webinar is different than if they attended either a traditional webinar or a Boardroom Briefing where I also presented.

This is down to what an attendee sees, and they see two things that are different.

Firstly, their view is different because instead of me sharing my screen and running through a PowerPoint or some other form of slide presentation, they see me standing in front of my E-Board in much the same way that they would view me if I were presenting at a physical seminar in a physical conference room.

Secondly, my E-Board is touchscreen enabled so I am able to use Visual Models combined with Open Loops just like I mentioned in the section above about Touch Screen Webinars. The difference is that, with an E-Board Webinar, they are seeing a giant digital white board because I'm not screen-sharing like I would be with the Touch Screen Webinar.

These two differences offer a tremendous advantage over the Traditional Webinar in terms of engagement levels, because the Audience member who has typically attended dozens if not hundreds of physical seminars and workshops is unconsciously experiencing something remarkably similar.

Remember what I said about our conference culture where we consider it rude to do anything other than pay the speaker careful attention?

Add to that the fact that the unconscious mind finds it difficult, if not impossible, to distinguish between two visual inputs that appear the same but that are in fact quite different.

What this means to you as the presenter is that your Audience pays much closer attention during an E-Board webinar than a Traditional Webinar because they feel uncomfortable with doing anything other than paying attention, *even if their webcams are off.*

An E-Board Webinar can give you the best of both worlds: it can give you the volume of Traditional Webinars and the engagement levels of a Boardroom Briefing Webinar and the captivation levels of a Touch Screen Webinar.

The downside with using an E-Board is there's a level of complexity that's added compared to any of the other webinar styles that I've just written about.

With a Traditional Webinar or a Touch Screen Webinar, the state of your office is irrelevant, so long as it's mostly soundproof. Your office could be a mess and it doesn't matter because no one gets to see it. The most important elements become having professional-looking slides, and an engaging style, plus a top-notch microphone.

(The latter which, by the way, is more important than quality graphics.)

Boardroom Briefings add a tiny layer of complexity over and above the Traditional Webinar because you have your webcam on and so you had better have a tidy background, preferably not one that's full of books where your Audience members are trying to read the titles from your library.

When you run any webinar with your webcam on, you want to have a plain vanilla background so that people's attention is either on you via your webcam or on your slides.

An interesting little side note on backgrounds: one of my clients began proudly running Boardroom Briefings with what she felt was an impressive looking library visible in the background. But she noticed some attendees were tilting their heads sideways trying to read the titles of the books and then starting to snigger.

One day she decided to check her library to find out what they were looking at, and to her horror she realized that she had a full and complete set of "50 Shades of Grey" (a series of books filled with sadomasochistic sexual exploits) lined up side-by-side occupying an entire shelf.

Oops.

Doubtless, she attracted some interest but maybe not for what she was hoping.

If Boardroom Briefings add a tiny layer of complexity due to needing a tidy background, and if Touch Screen Webinar add a bit more complexity due to the added technology required, then E-Board Webinars add a massive layer of complexity.

Firstly, attendees will not just see you and your E-Board. They will also be able to view to the left and right of your E-Board and they may also see above and below your E-Board.

That means you need to tidy up what will probably be a whole wall in your office and that's normally trickier if you have a home office.

In addition to that, you are going to require special lighting, otherwise the lighting on your ceiling and the natural lighting from a window will reflect off the screen of your E-Board and create what looks like sun flares.

And without great lighting, not only will it appear that your presentation has heat stroke, you will also appear quite dull and unenlightened (pun intended).

I touched on this briefly before, but it's worth repeating: most newcomers to marketing webinars fail to appreciate how important the audio quality is.

There's no doubt in my mind whatsoever that the audio quality is more important relative to engagement levels than the quality of your graphics.

If you're sitting at your desk presenting a webinar, you can have a desktop microphone of good quality (see Chapter Eight) but if you're standing three or four meters away from your webcam, then you will need a lapel microphone.

Also, there's more complexity when you present with an E-Board because you'll probably want to take advantage of the Captivation boost you get when writing by hand on the board and completing those lovely Open Loops and Visual Models.

There is absolutely no question that you will boost Captivation levels when you pick up a pen and start writing on the E-Board.

It's just the same as if you were presenting at a physical seminar or workshop and you picked up a pen and started writing on a flipchart or whiteboard.

People get intrigued.

They want to know what you are going to be writing, and added to that is the fact that any physical movement will draw attention to you as well.

It's just the way we human beings are wired. Let's work with what works.

Is investing in an E-Board worth it?

For me it certainly is.

For you, it's going to depend on your Audience.

Context is everything.

If I were marketing a $97 product to a small Audience of fishing enthusiasts, then an E-Board would not be worth the cost and complexity.

But if I were marketing the opportunity for a test flight in a private jet, then the answer would be a resounding "hell yes!"

CHAPTER EIGHT:

How to Choose the Right Platform and Technology for Your Webinar

IT'S NOT ABOUT THE BIKE

LANCE ARMSTRONG WON the Tour De France seven times and as everyone now knows, he did so with the aid of performance-enhancing drugs.

He's now a self-confessed cheat and to be fair, it's likely he confessed only when he knew the world was presented with evidence that made his previous denials hard to believe.

To continue by theme of fairness, most commentators agree that most of his competitors were also drug cheats. It seems that Lance Armstrong was not just a better cyclist, he was also a better cheat.

But let's leave the controversy of all that behind us and agree that every saint has their sins and every sinner has some redeeming features.

The point I want to make at the start of this chapter that features technology is emblazoned across the front of one of Lance Armstrong's best-selling books.

"It's Not About The Bike"

And even though I am a technology hog, marketing with webinars is not about the technology.

To reinforce the point that it's not about the technology, it would serve you well to know that when I started marketing with webinars, I didn't have a big budget.

I started with just my trusty old Lenovo laptop and for replays (not advisable these days, see Chapter Six) I used a free video platform that you may have heard of called YouTube.

I had a free email database account.

I had a low-budget webcam and I used the webcam's inbuilt microphone instead of a separate and better quality microphone.

I was in a home office and the extent of my lighting was limited to one bare lightbulb.

I used PowerPoint with free stock images and looking back, far too many bullet points with "death by PowerPoint" text and animations.

But I was still started pulling in more than $10,000 per webinar and that was way back in 2008.

These days, I have the best technology money can buy and sure, I'm generating a lot more revenue. But I tell you 100%, absolutely dead certain, that it's not about the technology.

For example, I have two giant 49-inch curved high definition Dell computer monitors. And I think I'm actually in love with them. Certainly, if love is spelled "t-i-m-e," as a relationship coach once told me, then I must be in love with them because I'm spending more time with them than with my wife.

Oops.

Did I just type that out loud?

I meant to just think it.

Moving on.

As mentioned earlier, behind me I also have a giant 75-inch Ultra High Definition (4k) E-Board.

And (he who has the most toys, wins) I also have a 4k boardroom conference webcam and a second 4k webcam for one-on-one meetings.

I'm subscribed to three webinar platforms because I serve both the small business and corporate market and they tend to be familiar with different platforms. So, I have them. But I don't actually need them.

I could go on about microphones and lighting and sound cards and speakers, tablets, tripods, backdrops and more.

But it's not about the bike. I only have all the tech toys because I love playing with it. But I don't need them all and you don't need them either.

It's not about the technology.

It's not about the technology.

It's not about the technology.

Did I mention that it's not about the technology?

Yes, the above is deliberately repeated because I can't emphasize it enough.

You can generate high quality, inbound, new client inquiries virtually every week of the year and you can do that without any significant cost or complication by following the recipe in this book.

Of course, you'll most likely accelerate your progress and you'll enjoy a much better result if you join one of my programs or work with me privately.

But that's beside the main point here which is this: please move forward with developing webinars as an additional or enhanced lead generation source regardless of your technology budget.

Sure, if you got a big fat bank account, then go ahead and indulge yourself with the tech toys. But if you're on a budget like I was when I started out, then move forward regardless.

At one stage, I was generating over $100,000 of fresh revenue every month, with big fat margins (because I was working from home), and I was doing that with an overhead of less than $200 each month. You can do the same.

It's more fun having technology toys but is not necessarily more profitable.

A general note on webinar platforms and technology

This chapter is not intended to offer you a comprehensive list of your platform and technology options.

Frankly, if I attempted that, the list would be out of date by the time the ink dried at the printers.

If not every day, then certainly every week, there are new apps, software, websites, platforms (I swear to God they create a new name for the same thing every other month) or whatever you want to call them, and some of them are brilliant and some of them are duds.

That's why I'm applying the 80/20 Principle to this chapter and simply recommending platforms and technology which are likely to still be around and still be great by the time you read this.

For the most part, I'm simply recommending what I use because I tend to be quite fussy and what I use has proven effective for me as a full-time professional webinar marketer and trainer.

That's not to say there are not other equally valid options out there for you.

WEBINAR PLATFORMS

My go-to platform for running traditional webinars is **www. GoToWebinar.com** for several reasons.

Firstly, I signed up for it in 2008 and GTW have honored the initial subscription fee that I commenced with, which means based on today's rates, I have a terrific deal because I accommodate 2,000 registrants for any one webinar for less than $100 a month.

But that's not the main reason I stuck with GTW.

Based on my experience with other platforms and what dozens of other professionals tell me, GTW is one of the most reliable platforms on the planet.

Thirdly, when I had a problem during a webinar, which has occurred only twice since 2008, I picked up the phone and a human being answered within three rings and that human being fixed the problem fast. That is exceptional customer service.

Fourth, GTW has one feature that I haven't seen any other platform which is their "Audience View" window.

If you have low or even moderate bandwidth, this feature is valuable. I'm not saying it is critical, but it is certainly helpful.

Audience View is a little window that I enlarge, that shows me in real time what my Audience is seeing. I doubt that it's 100% precise, but it's certainly a helpful guide.

The reason I like Audience view is that even if you have great bandwidth, there's always a small lag between when I change something on my screen and when my Audience is seeing that change.

Unless I synchronize my comments about what is changing on the screen with the moment that my Audience sees it, then I'm in danger of talking ahead of what they are seeing and they really have no idea what I'm talking about.

But because I see the changes when my Audience sees the changes, I synchronize my comments much more precisely.

Other webinar platforms that are high-quality and full-featured include **www.Zoom.us** (simple and easy to use), **www.twentythree.net** (brilliant in its simplicity and power), Microsoft Teams (for larger organizations), Cisco's **www.Webex.com** (ditto), Adobe's AdobeConnect (ditto again).

With the exception of TwentyThree, which I think is amazing and appears to be very robust, the others are all backed by massive companies and sadly, I find it difficult to endorse some of the smaller platforms due to ongoing reports of bugs and crashes.

PRESENTATION SOFTWARE

For Traditional Webinars I continue to use Microsoft's PowerPoint but there are certainly many other worthy contenders that I've heard great things about **www.haikudeck.com** , **www.prezi.com** and of course **www.canva.com.**

A variation to presentation slides are the apps that I mentioned in the previous chapter including **www.notability.com** (for Apple users only at time of writing) and Wacom's brilliant Bamboo Paper at **www.wacom.com/en-us/products/apps-services/bamboo-paper** available for Apple, Android, and Microsoft.

I've used the latter to enhance captivation during Touch Screen Webinars, filling in Open Loop and Visual Models (see Chapter Four).

Presentation Images

My go-to resource for world-class, professional looking images is **www.depositphotos.com,** but **www.unsplash.com** has a lot of free and impressive looking images too, and be sure to also check out **www.shutterstock.com**

Microphone

There are so many worthy contenders for quality microphones and they are like gloves. You just need to find one that fits you.

The one that I've stuck with for years now that has impressive quality for a very reasonable price is the Rode NT-USB microphone.

I have it mounted on my desk with the Rode desktop swing-arm and it therefore takes up no room on my desk and I can easily swing it close in front of my lips when I'm presenting, and away again when I'm done.

This is a very high-quality microphone for a relatively modest price and it's literally plug and play into a USB slot on your desktop, laptop, or tablet.

Webcam

For traditional webinars, you don't actually need a webcam, and other than turning it on for a brief introduction, it's probably more distracting than anything else, given that you want to direct people's attention toward your slides and not toward your nose.

For Boardroom Briefings, you need a webcam because you're going to be creating the expectation that every attendee has their webcam on. I have a Logitech Brio which is an Ultra High Definition (4K) webcam, and at time of writing, it's one of the very best available. And like the Rode microphone I mentioned above, it's a very good price relative to its quality.

For E-Board presentations, I use a Logitech MeetUp conference webcam that's designed for small boardroom conferences.

The reason I use this instead of simply using the Logitech Brio is because it comes with a remote control. I can zoom in and zoom out quickly and easily and that's really important when you're standing up in front of an E-Board because you don't want to have to be running back to your computer to adjust the width of view multiple times until you get it right.

Also, with the remote control, I can zoom in to just my head and shoulders at various times throughout the presentation and that increases the level of captivation, although my brother did once suggest that I had the perfect face for radio.

If you can get an Ultra High Definition (4K) webcam with a remote control that's not as expensive as Logitech's MeetUp, then I'd recommend that you do that, but at time of purchase, I couldn't find one.

SPEAKERS

Umm ... who cares?

I mean seriously, your Audiences don't.

They never hear them.

Still, got to have the tech, right?

I use a Soundblaster sound card with Razor Nommo speakers, but just use whatever you have because of all the technology, speakers are the least important.

OTHER HELPFUL, BUT NOT ESSENTIAL EQUIPMENT

One webinar format that I haven't mentioned in this book, simply for the sake of time, is the Boot Camp.

These are multi-day webinars and I have typically run them for an hour a day over five days.

The fifth day is where you make most of your sales.

I have run these successfully for a number of years, but several years ago, I ran one and on the fifth day a cyclone hit our little sleepy seaside suburb.

Our power was cut and so was our broadband Internet connection.

I couldn't run the webinar on the fifth day and that meant all the hard work of promoting and setting up and running the Boot Camp was almost a complete waste of time.

I say "almost" because there's always a residual effect to such events and some people who gain great value during the Boot Camp but then didn't have the opportunity to buy, will have purchased at a later date.

But from the Boot Camp itself, I got absolutely nothing.

Three purchases will prevent that from happening again, fingers crossed.

The first is what's referred to as a U.P.S. but you and I might know it as an uninterrupted power supply.

I purchased a CyberPower unit which is built like a battleship and feels half as heavy, which is hopefully a sign of quality engineering.

This device will power my desktop computer through a 60 minute webinar which is normally all I'd need.

For the tech heads who want to know, the model I settled on is the "3000VA CyberPower PRO Series Tower UPS with LCD PN PR3000ELCDSL."

The second is a simple gas fueled electricity generator.

The U.P.S. unit mentioned above will keep me running for 60 minutes or so without a problem, but after that, I'm going to need a generator. I have a Honda generator because they are among the quietest and are super reliable, plus they normally start with just one or two tugs of the starter rope.

The third item is an Internet router with a mobile phone Sim card, so that if my cable broadband goes down, the Sim card kicks in and I keep internet access connected via the mobile phone Sim card.

If however, the mobile phone tower gets wiped out, then I'm pretty much stuffed.

To be clear though, all of this is for the once-in-five-years cyclone or annual power outage.

The most important one of the three for me is definitely the U.P.S. device because it's all plugged in and if the power drops for any reason, cyclone's or otherwise, it automatically kicks in and keeps my computer and monitor and Internet router fully powered for more than 60 minutes.

EPILOGUE:

Your Options for Implementing the Ideas From This Book

A COMMON QUESTION THAT I get asked by my clients is how much of their intellectual property they should reveal during a webinar.

Their question comes from a concern about revealing too much of their "real oil."

It's quite understandable that you may also share a similar concern, which is that if you reveal too much, then your prospects might mistakenly believe that they can implement your ideas on their own.

Many years ago, I shared that concern and I followed the mantra of many marketers who say your book or seminar or webinar should tell people *what* they need to do but to also be explicit in communicating that they will need you to show them *how* to do it.

My conclusion after all these decades in marketing is that such an approach misses the mark by some margin. Read on to find out why.

Let me ask you this: is your ideal client a smart person with the money to pay for your services?

Of course, the answer is going to be a resounding "yes" and "yes."

That's because you don't want to work with people who don't have the intelligence to follow your recommendations, and because there is no point in you trying to work with people who can't afford you.

Therefore, it's axiomatic and inescapable that your ideal client will possess those two characteristics: they will be smart people who have enough money to work with you.

That being the case, let me assure you that if someone is smart and they have the money, they will not be tempted, for more than a fleeting moment, to try and implement on their own.

They will want to pay you money because they will want your help in implementing your methods and systems and processes and models, in whatever form they come, into their business or their life.

They are smart enough to understand that you will help them implement faster and more effectively, and that the money they pay you will be returned to them many times over, once they have implemented.

Yes, if they are stupid, they will try to implement on their own.

But I think we agree that you don't want to work with stupid people anyway.

You can help the ignorant, but it's impossible to help the stupid.

And if they can't afford you, then you are better to give them some valuable free content to help them until they can afford you.

Therefore, my recommendation is that you create your webinar to cater to the people who are smart and who also have the money to pay for your help in implementing and don't be concerned about giving too much away.

Just be sure that you are explicit and direct in communicating the fact that they will need you to help them implement.

In just the same way as I am doing here.

If you read this far, then there is a very high probability that you're both smart and that you have the budget to pay for me or one of my programs.

That's great news for both of us.

To that end, feel free to go and sign up for my SOLO program at **www.iWantSolo.com,** or if I have availability and you want to chat, you'll find a time here: **www.Book-AChatWithTom.com.**

And thanks again for investing in this book.

Best, Tom Poland

Chief Leadsologist.

Tom Poland Client Comments

I've gotten a much better return from my work with Leadsology than I have with any of the other professionals that I have given money to. Projecting where I a.m. going to be with my business within the next 12 months, I would say very conservatively three to five times what I've been earning on an annual basis prior to working with Tom."

Debora Hood, Hireometry
Denver, Colorado, USA

Use Leadsology because Tom is world-class in lead generation for coaches, consultants, and advisors. He absolutely knows his stuff and has a great way of teaching, coaching, and supporting the people that work with him
In terms of a return, it's multiples of what I've invested with Tom. I'm getting a hundredfold, if not a thousand fold, on my investment."

Shane Spiers, Mount Cook Associates
London, England

My market is CEOs and VPs of global food corporations. In the past, getting my message noticed by such senior people was difficult in the extreme.
But thanks to Leadsology® LeadStreams®, I now have a full pipeline of new client inquiries from Directors and C-Suite Execs of some of the world's biggest food corporations including Coke, Mars, and Unilever. To be honest, I'd never have thought this sort of result was possible and I'm relieved and delighted.

Derek Roberts, Consultant
Durban, South Africa

Prior to Leadsology® I was generating six figures, but almost killing myself scrambling around for clients.
I'm now having more fun, generating five times the number of new clients and in less time than I ever thought possible.

Christina Force, Coach and Trainer
Auckland, New Zealand.

During the first twelve months that I worked with Tom Poland our
revenue increased by 43 percent to over $1,000,000 and my net
personal earning's rose by 50 percent to $400,000.
We achieved the goals with no sacrifice of personal leisure time and we
continue to enjoy an "earnings per partner hour" which is amongst the
top quartile in the country.

Steve Bennet, Bennet and Associates
Whangerei, New Zealand

Leadsology will increase your business many times over. For the right
person who's willing to put in the work and the time, I don't think you
could find a better investment anywhere."
Anybody serious about increasing their business, getting in front of
more people that qualify for their business and are in the position to
make a decision, Tom is the way to go.

Terry Elder, USA Wealth First
Texas, USA

Since the Leadsology program, I have at least grossed in a six-digit
number based on the advice that Tom has provided over the years.
If I look at the amount of money that I've made from Tom's programs,
it goes without saying; that's a good deal."

Thomas Kessler, Blackboard M&A
Bonn, Germany

While I was working with Tom our turnover exploded, we
more than quadrupled our revenue and profits increased by
over 300 percent.
My investment with Tom has paid off more than tenfold. Tom's pro-
gram certainly delivers on its promises.

Ginny Scott, M.D. Capulet
Auckland, New Zealand

Thanks to Tom Poland's program, our profit has tripled. His
program is priceless. I couldn't put a price on where the program has
taken me from and where I a.m. now.

Dianne Bussey, FACT Solutions Consulting
Auckland, New Zealand

Prior to working with Tom Poland I was working long and hard but the business wasn't growing and I felt frustrated about that. **Thanks to working with Tom my business rapidly increased in value and is now worth millions.**

I can think of no reason why anyone who wants to add six or seven figures to their revenue would not apply to join Tom's program. My investment has paid off a thousand fold. Tom's program worked with me and I know of others who have had a similar result.

Win Charlebois, The Diamond Shop
Auckland, New Zealand

After joining Tom Poland's program **within nine months I've boosted profits and generated more revenue than the last three years put together.**

The actual overall improvement as a complete package in my business has been substantial and that's allowed me to become semi-retired.

Gilbert Chapman, Debt Recovery Group
Auckland, New Zealand

As a result of working with Tom Poland the value of my business increased by many millions of dollars. *My advice for any business owner who wants to enjoy more revenue and a better quality lifestyle, is to get on with it by joining Tom Poland's program.*

Grant Faber, Superbrokers Logistics Ltd
Auckland, New Zealand

Anything that doubles your income has got to be good and that's exactly what happened while working with Tom Poland.

Geoff Wilson, Professional Consulting Group
Auckland, New Zeland

Made in the USA
Middletown, DE
08 April 2022

63894884R00129